90-196

SCHOOL LIBRARY

Other Related Works

By The Author:

The Bounty Lands
Jonathan Blair:
Bounty Lands Lawyer
The Brooks Legend
Land Of the Inland Seas
The Cuyahoga

Other Midwest History

By The Publisher:

Early Flight
Cincinnati, Columbus, Cleveland & Erie
Railroad Guide
The Bounty Lands
Blue Jacket
The Cuyahoga
Time of Terror:
The Great 1913 Dayton Flood
Promises In The Attic
Dayton Sketchbook
Cincinnati Scenes

The Ordinance of 1787

The Nation Begins

by William Donohue Ellis

Landfall Press
Dayton, Ohio
1987

The Ordinance of 1787—The Nation Begins is officially recognized by the Ohio Northwest Ordinance and U.S. Constitution Bicentennial Commission.

With Gratitude

Besides the assistance of the many authors who researched different aspects of the development of the great ordinance, I am grateful for the assistance given this work by current scholars, librarians and curators:

Historian William Donnelly for reviewing the manuscript and for suggestions. Richard Cheski and Katherine Mead of the State Library of Ohio.

The staffs of Cleveland Public Library; Western Reserve Historical Society; Porter Public Library in Westlake, Ohio; Cahoon Library in Bay Village, Ohio; Molly Giles, North Olmsted Library; and Louise Zimmer, Washington County Public Library, Marietta, Ohio. John Briley, Executive Director, Campus Martius Museum, Marietta, Ohio. Dorothy A. Ellis, librarian.

Nancy A. Schneider for her work on every phase of the book.

Alex and Edith Kaye of Landfall Press. This publishing firm has made a specialty of preserving in print the heritage of the old Northwest Territory, and conceived this book.

W.D.E.

THE ORDINANCE OF 1787
The Nation Begins

by William Donohue Ellis

Copyright © 1987 by William Donohue Ellis

All rights reserved. Printed in the United States of America. No part of this book may be used or reproduced in any manner whatsoever without written permission of the Publisher, except in the case of brief quotations embodied in critical articles or reviews. For information please address Landfall Press, Inc., 5171 Chapin St., Dayton, Ohio 45429.

Library of Congress Catalog Card No. 87-061575
ISBN 0-913428-63-9 clothbound
ISBN 0-913438-64-7 paperback

*To Maude Donohue Ellis
My mother, raised on a
military bounty lands farm
in the West*

Those settlers in the first landing at Marietta:

Rufus Putnam, superintendent of colony
Col. Ebenezer Sproat, Surveyor
Major Anselm Tupper, Surveyor
John Matthews, Surveyor
Major Haffield White, Steward and Quartermaster

Captain Jonathan Devol	Benjamin Shaw
Captain Josiah Monroe	Jervis Cutler
Captain Daniel Davis	Samuel Cushing
Captain Peregrine Foster	Daniel Bushnell
Captain Jethro Putnam	Ebenezer Corry
Captain William Gray	Oliver Dodge
Captain Ezekial Cooper	Isaac Dodge
Phineas Coburn	Jabez Barlow
Daine Wallace	Allen Putnam
Gilbert Devol, Jr.	Joseph Wells
Jonas Davis	Israel Danton
Hezekiah Flint	Samuel Felshaw
Hezekiah Flint, Jr.	Amos Porter Jr.
Josiah Whitridge	John Gardner
Benjamin Griswold	Elizur Kirtland
Phiophilus Leonard	Joseph Lincoln
William Miller	Earl Sproat
Josiah White	Allen Devol
Henry Maxon	William Mason
William Moulton	Simeon Martin
Edmund Moulton	Peletiah White

(Col. Meigs did not arrive until 12 Apr 1788)

(Note the families: Devol, Sproat, Putnam, Cutler, Flint; and Matthews was a Putnam nephew.)

The other settlers arriving in 1788 were the following, making with the first 48 a total of 137:

Bozaleel Bryant
Ebenezer Battelle and family
Nathanial Cushing and family
James Converal
Frederick Crary
Lot Cheever
Asa Coburn and family
Luther Dana
Samuel Denney
Daniel Dunham and family
Samuel Dorrine
Sylvannus Eldridge
Oliver Fallen
Richard Greene
Charles Green and family
Major Nathan Goodale and family
William Gridley and family
Selah Hart
Holland
Ephraim Kimble
Theophilus Knight
John Lasa
William Lunt
Thomas Lord
Joseph Minot
John Mitchell
Jeffrey Matthewson
Neil McGuffey
Jar Owen
Stephen Pierce family
Robert Oliver family
Lancelot Oliver
Israel Putnam

Oliver Rice
John Stratton
John Skinner
Elias Stanley
Col. William Stacey and family
Benjamin Tupper family
Dan Tyler
Edward Tupper
James Varnum (died the next year)
Levi Woodward
Ebenezer Whittmore
James Backus
James Brayman
Benjamin Converse family
Archibald Crary
Joshua Cheever
Jeffrey Chaouchip
William Dane family
Edmund Dane
Nathan Dicks
Cornelius Delano
Richard Elliott
Paul Fearing
Griffin Greene family
Philip Green
Jonathan Gilbert
Tim Goodale
Benoni Hurlburt family
Thomas Hutchinson
George Ingersoll
Charles Knowles
Hamilton Keri
Ezra Lunt

James Leach
Dick Laughton (half Indian)
John Miles (half Indian)
Samuel Mitchell
Abel Mathews
Nathanial Moody family
Ichabod Nye family
Samuel H. Parson
Alexander Oliver family
William Oliver
Waldo Putnam

Winthrop Sargent
Samuel Stratton
Jonathan Stone family
Samuel Stebbins
Joshua Shipman family
Jobez True
Judah Tupper (died in war)
Benjamin Tupper Jr.
Simeon Wright
Andrew Webster family

Contents

Chapter 1: Washington	15
Chapter 2: Pickering	25
Chapter 3: Putnam	33
Chapter 4: Mr. Jefferson and Mr. Monroe	41
Chapter 5: Tupper	53
Chapter 6: The General	63
Chapter 7: Cutler	73
Chapter 8: The Compact	87
Chapter 9: The Land Buyer	93
Chapter 10: Company Business	105
Chapter 11: Putnam	109
Index	117
Other Reading	120
The Ordinance of 1787 text	124

Introduction

On the 13th day of July 1787, the Congress under the Articles of Confederation adopted "An Ordinance for the Government of the Territory of the United States Northwest of the River Ohio." Determined not to make the mistakes that England had made in her treatment of 13 former colonies, the new United States in establishing its first colony — the Northwest Territory, between the Ohio and Mississippi Rivers and the Great Lakes — put in place the most magnanimous colonial policy the world had ever seen.

Even the words "colony" and "colonial" with their connotations of subservience would be absent in the new Ordinance, replaced by the words "territory" and "territorial." Assured to those who would settle in the Northwest Territory, in six Articles of Compact (sometimes called the First Bill of Rights), were freedoms which even residents in many of the original 13 seaboard states did not yet enjoy. The Northwest Territory, or Old Northwest as it would come to be called, was destined to become "Freedom's Proving Ground."

It was Franklin D. Roosevelt who called the Northwest Ordinance of 1787 "that third great charter...the highway over which poured the westward march of our civilization...the plan on which the United States was built." He was right.

With the Declaration of Independence and the Constitution, the Ordinance was indeed the "third great charter" in the formation of our nation. And it was the plan by which a tiny eastern seaboard nation of 13 states could grow to 50 continental states and beyond, each one equal to the others, a plan still in effect as seen in the territories of Samoa and the Marianas today.

Of the three great charters in our history it is the Ordinance which has the least name recognition, which is the least understood. One explanation for this is the incredibly complex, unappealing and legalistic style in which much of it is written, a fault not shared by the other two documents. Though the Confederation Congress had considered the measure for more than three years, it was modified extensively and completed in haste in a single week, 6-13 July 1787. Quite simply, it reflects the haste in which it was written.

Another explanation is that it had no primary authors of first rank to give it stature and nobility. The immortality of a Thomas Jefferson, an Alexander Hamilton or a Benjamin Franklin would not embrace this document as the Declaration and the Constitution were embraced. Instead, the Ordinance was the creature of a succession of committees, principle figures of which were men of lesser rank and lesser command of language.

Yet a third explanation is that the Ordinance was the product of a dying Congress scarcely able to function under the ineffective Articles of Confederation. This contrasted sharply with the excitement attending the birth of a new nation with the Declaration of Independence and the birth of a new government under the Constitution of the United States.

Finally, the Ordinance was tarnished by the spectre of speculation. The principal reason for its passage that July 1787 was the near bankruptcy of the federal treasury and the availability of ready cash from speculative land companies eager to take advantage of that distress by negotiating the purchase of great chunks of the public domain for pennies on the acre once government in the territory had been established.

Consequently, the Ordinance has never had quite the aura of idealism and virtue about it that it perhaps deserves and which has been associated with the Declaration or the Constitution. Nor till now, on its 200th anniversary, has it had much scholarly attention.

Why, then, in light of all its shortcomings do we find modern historians in general agreement on its greatness, its abiding place of honor among all American institutions? Bruce Catton, in his final work published posthumously, *The Bold and Magnificent Dream,* spoke for many when he wrote of the Ordinance:

"Once and for all, it determined what kind of country this was going to be; the concept of complete equality, so nobly voiced in the Declaration, was written into the basic document that would determine how the nation grew. It compelled men to look past their own dooryards to something unlimited beyond the horizon, and decreed that a man's place as a member of the American Republic would be forever greater than his place as a resident of a single state..."

There has long been a need for a book for the general audience, for the non-historian and the student of history alike, to tell the story of the Northwest Ordinance of 1787 in graphic, narrative terms to enable it to come alive, that it might be understandable and readable despite the incredibly complex style in which the Ordinance itself was written.

This is such a book, written by William Donohue Ellis, one of the midwest's finest writers and historians. It deserves to be read. It is an important contribution to the bicentennial commemoration of America's third great charter and the proving ground of freedom which emerged from it.

>Phillip R. Shriver
>President Emeritus and Professor of History, Miami University
>Chairman, Ohio Bicentennial Commission for the Northwest Ordinance and the United States Constitution

Foreword

Ordinance: (L. ordinare — to put in order)
"We must put our house in order." The tired general at Mt. Vernon was fighting personal debt and severe rheumatism in early 1787. But more disabling to him was watching the exploding dissolution of the headless ungoverned confederation of arrogant, warring states. "Thirteen sovereignties pulling against each other will soon bring ruin on the whole."

And so, at 55 years, the general reluctantly headed his coach north to Philadelphia once more, this time to the Federal (Constitutional) Convention to "put our house in order."

"We have a national character to establish (...) to prevent being made the sport of European policy."

In the same summer, a Massachusetts doctor representing The Ohio Company of Adventurers drove his surrey south to make a proposal to the Continental Congress, meeting in New York.

His proposal would result in the Ordinance of 1787, generally considered America's third most important document. It would put our house in order, setting the method of development and "a national character" of the future development of this nation.

The doctor rode home to Massachusetts, carrying that Ordinance which committed Congress to act as a united government in creation of new states to be united with the old "on an equal footing." Parts of this ordinance would be adopted by the men in Philadelphia who were writing a constitution. The doctor left others to finalize his land contract for a new state.

The general rode home to Mt. Vernon, carrying a copy of the Constitution, leaving the Committee on Style to make a few eleventh-hour modifications. The big change they made was the first one. The Preamble began: "We, the people of the states of..." naming all the states. The Committee scratched that and penned in: "We the people of the United States."

The house was in order.
William Donohue Ellis
Cleveland, Ohio
July, 1987

Chapter 1: Washington

"The Touch Of A Feather May Turn It Any Way."

"Good God!" The tired general was addressing Henry Knox, war secretary, "Who besides a Tory could have foreseen or a Briton predicted this?"

In some anger, but more with a searching sadness the former general-in-chief of the Continental Army considered the latest report of the dissolution of the Confederation which he thought the army had locked together six years ago when the smoke settled at Yorktown.

At 55 the long-striding frame still reminded visiting petitioners of the stalking silhouette in the gunsmoke between tattered guidons. But now it flinched frequently with the rheumatism that pricked his confidence in his own performance of the public services still demanded of him. Five hundred pounds of debt, 340 of it for taxes, worried him. The loss of his close brother, John Augustine, left him without an off-parade companion. His mother's financial whining harried him. The jowls had thickened some but the granite profile still glared out over his people, stern and concerned.

This latest worry forecasting the probable dissolution of the Confederation in 1787 was Captain Shays' massive New England rebellion by debtor war veterans. Threatening to explode New England and New York, it was only the latest straw in Washington's view of the Confederation shattering into 13 warring nations and chaos.

Captain Daniel Shays, a dynamic battle-scarred natural leader,

(1787)

reluctantly but aggressively led an uprising of about 1200 against the courts and the federal armory at Springfield, Massachusetts, to force relief from debtor laws.

British propaganda was informing crown loyalists that the British troops in the nine Great Lakes forts were standing by to become an army of occupation when the young American republic collapsed.

The general remembered the day he broke the seal of the envelope handed him by the blindfolded British officer:

Sir: I propose a cessation of hostilities (. . .) to settle terms for the surrender of the posts at York and Gloucester. I have the honour to be &c

Cornwallis

It had been a miracle. The precarious confederation had held together just well enough, while losing the battles, to win the war against the greatest military power on earth. But no sooner had we won from the British the western reach of the continent than the individual states claimed vast western stretches of it under colonial charters from the crown they had just defeated.

Washington warned Knox, "There are combustibles in every state which a spark might set fire to." He now feared the break up of the Confederation.

He had reason.

For six years since the surrender the victory had hung on a thread.

The Confederation was immediately so bankrupt that there was not enough money available to pay the expenses of Tench Tilghman for carrying the message of the surrender to Congress. The delegates unpocketed a dollar each to make up the difference.

The British hardly defeated, the confederated states turned on each other, separate nations. Several maintained their own navies. Massachusetts sent to the Continental Congress not a representative but an ambassador from the sovereign Massachusetts, now raising its own army. States instituted tariffs against each other. Virginia empowered her citizens to capture for booty any customs-evading vessels of other states. Pennsylvania and Connecticut fought a shooting war.

The small states feared the large.

Congress had no power to collect taxes, only to request contributions. Young Alexander Hamilton repeatedly published notice in New York papers: "The subscriber has received nothing on account of the quota of the state for the present year." Rhode Island refused to pay. New Hampshire had not paid one shilling since the peace and "does not ever mean to pay."

The Articles of Confederation, merely a voluntary agreement formed under enemy attack, became a rope of sand with the enemy's retreat.

The Congress was a forceless non-government, unlike any in history, over a loose league of colonies. The headless Confederacy, with no president, could request but not demand. It had no fund to pay congressmen. States could send two to seven delegates as they pleased, or none. Usually no more than nine states were represented.

Washington, Hamilton, Madison and other giants of the Revolution pressed for a constitution to establish a strong central government. But the idea of a constitution and a national government was despised by the people who had just overthrown one. The anemic Articles of Confederation would have to do. These Articles, largely commercial, kept the Congress weak.

"For heaven's sake," protested Washington, "where are the Congress? Are they not the creatures of the people? (...) What can be the danger in giving them such powers as are adequate?"

Worse, while these 13 nations quarreled, unable to govern even the eastern seaboard, France, Spain and England eyed expectantly the vast lands west of the Appalachian ridge, as did the individual states who intended to own it.

The general protested to Governor Randolph of Virginia, that the country, *"stands on a pivot — the touch of a feather may turn it any way."*

The Feather Arrives

On the fifth day of July in that same year, 1787, a genial 45-year-old doctor drove south in a sulky from Massachusetts to visit the Congress in New York. Although he had a very heavy mission, he had a touch as light as a feather.

He came to buy a state.

His trip produced a written contract that tipped the continent on its pivot.

Folded twice to form a slim document, 4½ inches across, 7¾ inches tall, turning brown around the edges, one copy at this writing is traveling the United States under guard along with the Magna Carta. The brown ink on the cover announces:

> *An Ordinance for the Government*
> *of the Territory of the United*
> *States Northwest of the Ohio River.*
> *Chas. Thompson*
> *Secretary of Congress*
> *July 13, 1787*

Although the title specified the Northwest Territory, it turned out to be for the territory between the Atlantic and Pacific and Alaska and Hawaii.

Another original copy is treasured by Marietta College, Marietta, Ohio.

The trigger copy was the one sledged down the snow-crusted Tuscarora slope of the Allegheny range by 26 men and their horses. Although this advance party of The Ohio Company of Associates only wanted to start a new state, *what they started was a unified single nation, with a plan for holding the continent, where previously there had been a collection of 13 sovereignties barely holding onto a 200 mile deep coastal shelf.*

The Treaty of Paris did not hand us possession of the 3,000 mile continental width. West of the mountains was coveted expectantly by the British generals who retained their western garrisons and

Indian allies, by the French, by the Spanish and by the sovereignties of Connecticut, Massachusetts, New York, Virginia, the Carolinas and Georgia, who claimed "the backlands" under their old charters from British kings who had written colonial western boundaries loosely..."extending west from sea to sea."

Colonial attorneys now interpreted that to mean the Pacific or at least the Mississippi.

The colonizing *scheme* of The Ohio Company gave birth to the Ordinance of 1787. They were cause and effect.

The Ordinance in turn expedited the Constitution, which was stalled in a stand-off, East against West ["I (...) despair of seeing a favorable issue to the proceedings (...)." — Washington].

The Ordinance

The document has two parts. The first ordains the kind of government to be erected and the way the lands would be divided into states, counties and townships, the stages of progression in status from territory to state.

The second part, made up generally of six major ideas, is six articles of compact "to forever remain unalterable" between the people of the original states and the people of the future states.

Although all of the ideas are profound, the one new key concept that made the nation flow to the west coast — as opposed to all history's then failed colonization schemes — was the provision that as new states were formed they would be brought into the union *"on an equal footing"* with the parent states with equal representation.

That pivotal idea, the basis of the fiercest arguments, appeared first in the ordinance, then followed in the Constitution.

It seems so obvious, now, but none of the great colonizers had grasped it. Not Rome, Britain, Spain, Holland, Portugal, France. And in the Federal Convention arguing in Philadelphia, just across New Jersey from the Congress in New York, that equality for new colonies was a hated, radical concept. From his chair, wooden leg stretched out in front, the genial, handsome Gouverneur Morris, was pulling the Constitutional Convention his way, "...we should govern them as provinces, and allow them no voice in our councils."

Elbridge Gerry, shrewd New England merchant, whined new back country states will "drain our wealth into western country." He wanted to curtail creation of new states so that "they shall never outnumber the Atlantic states." Rufus King of Massachusetts seconded that.

Grouped around Morris against the back country was a powerful block — Butler; Clymer; Rutledge; the respected Elbridge Gerry; and young, balding, and politically experienced Rufus King. Relentless against equality for new states was the abusively aggressive Marylander, one of the country's most feared and successful lawyers (he would defend Aaron Burr), Luther Martin.

These strong men wanted no state created in the west, only dependent colonies. They had a case.

They argued that already an ungovernable stream of squatters straggling west was creating lawless small nations with permission from no one — Transylvania, Westsylvania, Franklin, Vandalia, and Transallegheny West. They had no allegiance to the eastern seaboard nor to any flag.

Expounding that argument with his stone-grinding voice and country-boy cunning, Rufus King's heavy pacing punished the floor planks in Philadelphia. But he knew that at the very same time across New Jersey in New York the feeble Congress was working on a document to the contrary, the Ordinance of 1787.

The Nation's Most Important Ordinance

Governments produce thousands of ordinances. Why is this one considered America's most important ordinance and third most important document after the Declaration of Independence and the Constitution? Why is it being traveled across the nation under guard to be viewed by the people?

First — its appearance at that moment forced a turning point. Suddenly the unharnessed collection of nation states made, as a single teamed entity, history's largest contract, "forever —

unalterable." That contract, even before we had a constitution, pledged that new states would be "admitted on equal footing."

The Ordinance helped force the ratification of the Constitution by the states. For example it was young Hamilton's most effective weapon in coercing a stubborn New York assembly.

Second — the concepts carried in its few hundred words, set the character of the future nation.

What concepts?

The Ordinance created the system for territories and procedures for them to develop into full-fledged states with equal representation in national government.

It mandated a system for measuring and assigning the lands.

It provided for public education, including higher education.

It mandated religious freedom, abolition of involuntary servitude and slavery and abolition of the ancient primogeniture custom under which estates descended to the eldest son.

It mandated the right of habeas corpus, trial by jury of peers, the right of private property and the sanctity of private contracts.

That was the "national character" and the union which Washington said was imperative — a code for America.

These concepts it established in advance of completion of the Constitution; and many of these concepts would find their way from the Ordinance into the Constitution.

Why did a weak Congress suddenly produce this internationally superb code?

Sudden wisdom? Sudden altruism?

Perhaps. But history shows us that a man suddenly drove into New York from Massachusetts to present the Congress the largest business opportunity it had ever seen. He represented The Ohio Company of Associates. He asked for certain conditions, and he had the authority to negotiate immediately. Further, he had a certain flair about him.

Who Created The Ordinance?

Gallons of printer's ink and tons of paper in learned journals have debated authorship of this enshrined document, particularly Article VI forbidding involuntary servitude. Various advocates claim it for Nathan Dane, Edward Carrington, Manasseh Cutler, Richard Henry Lee and others. Often the arguments have been passionately parochial, depending upon where the advocate lived.

Two hundred years of perspective show us that the Great Ordinance was drafted by at least a thousand men. No more than we could credit the winning of the Revolution to the last 20 infantrymen firing at Yorktown can we credit the last 20 men involved with the Ordinance of 1787. Its authors go back 100 years before that to relays of Virginia burgesses and Massachusetts selectmen pressing for relief from governor generals.

Some of the principles in the Ordinance illuminated previously written state constitutions nearly in the same language and also other documents in which men attempted to seize simple justice.

While the Ordinance seemed to be written and approved in eight days between July 5th and 13th, 1787, it was actually fought out over nearly six centuries and many generations from its great grandfather's great grandfather — the Magna Carta of year 1215.

Just one example of the direct descent:

Magna Carta
Chapter 39, 1215

No freeman shall be taken, imprisoned, disseized, outlawed, or in any way destroyed, nor will we proceed against him, except by lawful judgement of his peers, and by the law of the land.

Ordinance of 1787
Article II

The inhabitants (...) shall always be entitled to the benefits of habeas corpus, and of trial by jury (...). All persons shall be bailable, unless for capital offences (...). No man shall be deprived of his liberty or property but by the judgement of his peers, or the law of the land.

Who created the Ordinance? It is a collection of ancient wisdoms for governance, distilled from centuries and assembled on one page, folded.

With its expiring breath the Confederation Congress gave us this ordinance — of reason, good will and simple justice for settling and governing a huge new land. Then this Congress of 18 to 25 men adjourned, never to meet again.

How could that hostile climate produce this code for America? It began in anger in 1783.

Dayton-Montgomery County Public Library

Timothy Pickering

Chapter 2: Pickering

(1783)

Enroute to his office in the awkward walk of a crippled crane, lank Col. Timothy Pickering, quartermaster general, skirts the main bivouac area of Newburgh. In this demobilization camp on the Hudson troops grouse miserably around fires in a sharp spring. With the preliminary peace treaty signed, Congress wants the army to go home; but the troops are waiting for discharge pay. The sullen Newburgh camp is a finger-wagging scold reproaching the leadership. Especially the men watch Pickering.

The man who is most personally the target of the poverty of the Confederation at the close of the Revolution is probably this Colonel Pickering of Salem, Massachusetts.

A sharp-edged man with busy eyes too close astride a blade of a nose, Pickering is a package of turmoil. Incessant ambition, which he clothes as righteousness, is thwarted by unconcealed envy. A perennial staff type in the shadows of the great combat generals, he served them throughout the war and politicked among them for advancement. But from the moment of Cornwallis' message to Washington, "Sir, I propose cessation of hostilities..." the senior generals relaxed in a series of ceremonials and dumped the ugly closing down of the war partly onto Pickering's bony shoulders.

That meant facing war's enormous debts — with no funds.

He so resented the assignment that he traveled to Congress demanding his salary be doubled or he would quit. Congress halved his salary and sent him back to work.

Pickering became hardened to turning away creditor merchants, manufacturers, mercers, ironmongers and armorers. At war's end these creditors struck army headquarters like the rainlash after the hurricane. They reminded Pickering how only months before he had begged them for war supplies, convincing each the whole war's outcome was in his hands.

He could remind them they had lost no blood. But what Pickering could not face down were the stares of these troops awaiting demobilization and pay. Although Pickering had been a staff man, he had seen the blood flow as Washington's adjutant in the Jersey campaigns. He knew what these men had endured. And now he could not decently clothe nor even feed them as they awaited discharge pay. Pickering had no pay for them.

"To hear the complaints (...) and see the miserable condition of the soldiery (...) penetrates my inmost soul to see men destitute of clothing, who have risked their lives (...) having large arrears of pay due them and prodigiously pinched for provisions."

In begging Congress for provisions and money Pickering pleaded that many of the men..."have for six years exposed their lives to save their country (...) have for a month past been destitute of every comfort (...)."

Sloshing through the camp in the night Pickering overheard the mood that leaked from the tents in the wood smoke. One gravel voiced captain with seven years service exploded to a huddle of officers, "If this is your treatment while your swords are necessary for the defense of America, what have you to expect from peace when (...) no remaining mark of military distinction is left you but your wants, infirmities and scars? Can you then consent to be the only sufferers by this revolution, and (...) grow old in poverty and contempt? (...) Then go starve and be forgotten."

A group of officers petitioned the Congress for back pay, "We have bourne all that man can bear. Our property is expended, our private resources are at an end, our friends are wearied out and disgusted with our incessant applications. We therefore most seriously and earnestly beg that a supply of money be forwarded to the army (...)."

Anger spread through the army like pigweed in a wet spring. A trouble-rousing Col. Robert Stewart came into Newburgh with the story that Congress intended to adjourn leaving the troops unpaid. One contingent of Pennsylvania officers marched troops on Congress, demanding money. Congress fled to Princeton.

To pay those creditors who threatened withholding food from camp, Pickering sold off army property — wagons, guns and tents. To officers who had given up on getting paid and were going home, Pickering sold army dragoon horses so the officers would not have to walk home.

But selling army property did not begin to hold off the war's big creditors.

Final Certificates

The Confederation had no choice but to issue pieces of paper, certificates of settlement, interest-bearing warrants on a bankrupt treasury, to be honored someday, possibly.

They came to be called *final certificates* or *finals*.

Destitute holders of these certificates traded them on the open market for necessities. The deluge of these finals shrank their value to one-sixth face value. "One in six" was the seller's demand in any negotiation. Everything had two prices, paper or coin.

Bounty Land Warrants

Many soldiers held bounty land warrants awarded as a bonus by Congress, September 15, 1776, to men who would sign up for three year enlistments instead of three months. In addition, Virginia issued her own bounty land warrants to her own troops. All of these bounty land warrants were to be good for acreage in the West...if we won the war. But these western lands were not yet available for the central government to give to the veterans. The lands were claimed by the individual states. Some destitute discharged veterans were already trading away these warrants at twenty cents on the acre.

The Army Plan

Caught in this financial ambush, officers capable of surviving Stony Point and Monmouth and Verplanck Point were naturally going to seek some escape route.

In pursuing that self interest, they would plant a concept larger than their own goal.

A group of Newburgh officers remembered that in the depths of the war on several nights when General Washington felt they might be overrun at dawn by well-equipped British, he had told his commanders to tell their troops, "If the war should fail, the soldiers should withdraw west of the Alleghenies into the Ohio Valley and live in freedom."

Therefore in 1783 when, though they had won the war they had lost it, some officers at Newburgh dreamed a plan to create a new state. It would lie west of Pennsylvania between the Ohio River and the Erie Lake, extending west to the Great Miami and the Maumee Rivers.

Colonel Pickering definitely took a very active role, how much is not clear, but he is the one who wrote down the ideas of the officers and carried on the correspondence. It began to be called *The Pickering Plan*, sometimes the *Army Plan*, later the *Newburgh Plan*.

The basic idea was that the government buy from the Indians that huge tract and that it become a new state, and that these lands be sold to this group of veterans in exchange for their *bounty land* warrants as originally prescribed by Congress in 1776:

To a	acres		acres
Major General	1100	Lieutenant	200
Brigadier	850	Ensign	150
Colonel	500	Non-Commissioned	100
Lieutenant Colonel	450	Soldier	100
Major	400	Surgeon	400
Captain	300	Surgeon's Mate	300

And for any soldier who would actually settle the land within one year of the purchase from the Indians, the acreage would double, plus 50 acres for each additional member of his family.

The officers proposed that for the security of the new state and the nation against Indians, each soldier-settler be required to go armed and serve in the new state's militia.

Pickering wrote it all down. And by letters he recruited officers stationed elsewhere, "(...) a new plan is in contemplation — no less than the forming of a new state westward of the Ohio (River). Some of the principal officers are heartily engaged in it. About a week since the matter was set on foot and a plan is digesting for the purpose. Enclosed is a rough draft of some propositions respecting it which are generally approved of."

There was a neatly penned title on the enclosure:

"Propositions for Settling a New State by Such Officers and Soldiers of the Federal Army as Shall Associate for that Purpose."

Some of those propositions were these. The new state's constitution would totally exclude slavery. The settlers would form a state government with representation in the Congress. They proposed rules for governance, for care of the poor, for education, rules of conduct and finally admission to the union as an *equal* state.

The officers prefaced the final draft with a petition to Congress signed by 285 men.

But this was only a paper signed by destitute officers who did not cut deep tracks in congressional politics.

To Reach A Deaf Congress

These officers were, however, sophisticated enough to know that the Congress was under siege from all the urgent grief in war's wake. That included insistent petitions from several other military groups with similar plans for paying the army with land. Besides, Congress was comprised of men whose own private lives and financial affairs had also been destroyed. All men were cheated equal.

And the membership of Congress constantly rotated. Trying to get Congress' attention was like grabbing fog.

Congress, disenchanted with the army, a giant, frightening problem, wanted the army disbanded.

Only one soldier in the nation now could command the Congress' attention to a large request from military people. General Washington.

But every supplicant had the same idea. Therefore the general — tired, in debt, and eager to tend farm — was as besieged as Congress by imperative needs of a new nation. All the urgencies postponed by war now slammed due with foreclosure force. And the Olympian general, already one of history's handful, was the target of every problem. If he never slept he had not time even to hear or read all petitions presented him.

Who among the officers could best outrank the clamor for Washington's attention and enlist him to advocate this Pickering Plan to Congress?

Why not Pickering?

Pickering had made the mistake of many bright senior officers. While serving as Washington's adjutant in the field, Pickering confided to General Greene that before joining the staff he had "an exalted opinion of General Washington's military talent. But I have since seen nothing to enhance it." Again, ignoring Washington's daring strokes at Trenton and Princeton, he commented, "The general does want decision." It was discovered later that, though the general could spare no time to quash all the rear echelon knifing by scores of his ambitious officers, he was aware and sensitive to it.

After Pickering had become quartermaster general, Washington on one occasion needed at the front certain supplies which, on the excuse of unavailability, were not arriving. However, Washington had seen some stockpiles in the rear. He dropped his famous reserve and warned Pickering, "The time is come when these things must be done and the execution rests with you. For whenever it shall be known that these provisions were in the neighborhood and that the troops suffered for want (...) the whole blame (...) will be attributed (...) to your department."

When Washington was finally enroute home, top officers asked him to stop off at West Point that they might deliver a response to his famous Farewell Address. Three officers composed the address to Washington, one being Pickering. He argued for making it brief and "not stuffing it with fulsome adulation." He resisted the other two on including the word "magnanimity," shrinking it to "prudence," later bragging that he held the speech to "moderate." Thus the great commander's final tribute was written by a detractor.

Pickering was not the right envoy to Washington.

Then which officer could powerfully recruit the general's advocacy of the Pickering Plan?

There were some available. But one particularly had everyone's trust...including Washington's.

Dayton-Montgomery County Public Library
Rufus Putnam

Chapter 3: Putnam

Compared to the galaxy of stellar senior generals besieging Congress for favors and back pay in post-war Philadelphia, Rufus Putnam was a minor, only named brigadier at war's end.

Stout, with a sloping dewlap from chin to tunic, he was a plain man among such flamboyant figures as his own admired relative, General Israel Putnam.

Yet Putnam's plainness was his force. Walking like a bull penguin he faced the political gods with his head up in country dignity. A man undivided by uncertainties, he brought his whole history on his face. You looked at him — you knew him. And you were compelled to look because of a slight eye injury which turned his head a half notch.

Between Putnam and General Washington were many levels of epaulet colors, and the larger gap between Yankee farmer and Virginia planter. And yet they were alike.

Like Washington, Old Put was never young. His father died when he was seven. His new stepfather, Captain Saddler, put him to work in the inn in Sutton, Massachusetts, and faulted him for wasting his tip money on arithmetic books. He bound out Rufus at 16 to a millwright.

Like Washington, Putnam had been at war since upper boyhood. He broke indenture at 19 in 1757, signing on with the British Ranger Scouts.

Like Washington, from that first hitch he had been in and out of various combat units, alternating military with civilian work, in Putnam's case farming, surveying and building grinding mills.

Before he ever saw Washington in the great rebellion, Colonel Putnam had already fought with the British on the upper Hudson, Lake Champlain and in the freezing campaign near Ft. Edwards. He witnessed Indian butchery of comrades and survived the overwhelming of Fort Henry by Montcalm's French-Indian army.

He reenlisted with the Royal Regulars against the French at Lake George, and again under General Amherst against Fort Ticonderoga.

When the British attacked across the Old North Bridge at Concord, Massachusetts, in 1775, Putnam signed on as a light colonel in Brewer's regiment at Roxbury, Massachusetts, under the guns of the British, and unfortified except for a board fence.

In a council considering the defense, a General Heath suggested to commanding General Thames that there was a light colonel Putnam who had engineering experience and had built flour mills.

Summoned by Thames to fortify Roxbury for defense, Putnam replied that he had "never read a rod on the subject of fortification. It is true that I (...) some work of that sort under British engineers, but I pretended to no knowledge in (...) laying out works."

But Thames had stone ears.

Putnam, applying common sense, laid out and superintended construction of works at Roxbury, Cobble Hill and proximate points.

The general-in-chief of the armies was coming to inspect the works. Tensing the commander's arrival in New England to take charge of the rebellion were two hostile currents. Massachusetts, being first to shed blood under the king's attack, felt that a Massachusetts man should head the Continental Army. Congress, prodded by pragmatic John Adams, in order to enlist the support of southern troops, elected instead a southerner, one G. Washington.

Arriving in Boston to take charge of the action, the general felt the Yankee chill. He was already aware that many of his top staff here considered themselves better qualified than he, and expected to displace him. The general thickened the frost by his obvious disappointment in New England troops, their casual discipline, unprofessionalism, and insubordinate Yankee arrogance.

He was accustomed to the more professional southern military tradition.

Therefore when the general inspected the Putnam defense works at Roxbury, he was relieved at their professionalism and that of the veteran lieutenant colonel in charge. He requested Putnam to make surveys and maps for building the army's works in nearby Cambridge.

In the winter of 1776, Washington was planning how to dislodge the British from Boston. One particular evening bonded a tacit trust between two plain men. The challenge before the staff at evening mess in Cambridge was that British General Howe's army of 11,000 backed by strong supply from his fleet in the harbor, were in position to storm Boston. Washington preferred the showdown occur instead over on Dorchester Heights. He wanted to move troops there so that Howe would attack him there, risking another Bunker Hill battle, but one the Americans could win. If Washington's troops could fortify themselves on the land neck between Boston and Dorchester they would command both Boston and the harbor.

However, Dorchester Heights, frozen so hard that it bounced pickaxes, could not be fortified with earthworks.

No solution developed at table. Washington dismissed the officers, signaling Putnam to remain. He asked Putnam to think intensively about the Dorchester Heights maneuver, and report immediately if he could invent a way to dig defensive works.

Putnam started for his quarters with a friend who had waited. Passing one general's quarters, Putnam said "Let's call on General Heath."

He intended a casual visit, but once inside Putnam noticed a book, *Muller's Field Engineer*. He immediately said to Heath, "Lend it to me."

Heath refused.

Putnam said his need of the book was urgent.

"I never lend my books."

Putnam reports, "I then told him he must recollect that he was the one who, at Roxbury (...) compelled me to undertake a business which, at that time, I confessed I had never read a word about, and that he must let me have the book. After some more excuses on his part and close pressing on mine, I obtained the loan of it."

Back in his quarters next morning, Putnam was reading the table of contents. A new word jumped out at him — *chandeliers*.

He turned to the page and studied with excitement. Washington's entrenchments would be above ground!

On the reverse slope, out of sight of the enemy, Putnam put the men to building chandeliers. To build each chandelier the troops cut a stout timber ten feet long. Into this they set uprights five feet high, five feet apart. Aligning two of these frames in parallel a yard apart and connected by light timbers, they filled the gap with tightly bundled branches, *fascines*. Out of sight of the enemy, the men built a long row of these chandeliers, with no give-away clue but the fragrance of fresh sawn apple wood.

At dusk, March 4, 1776 the British looked up from their ships at Dorchester Heights and retired for the night confident the colonists could not defend that terrain.

When the dark pushed out the day, the Americans slid the chandeliers up the icy reverse slope of Dorchester Heights, over the brow, and down the forward slope just enough so that riflemen's heads above the chandeliers would not be silhouetted above the ridge line.

On the morning of March 5th, General Howe awoke and stared inland through the mist as usual. Startled, his eyes made out a long American fortification along Dorchester Heights, apparently built overnight.

Supporting these infantrymen formidably were 58 cannon which General Henry Knox had hauled from Ft. Ticonderoga in an historic logistics maneuver.

Howe sent a message to Lord Dartmouth, that to accomplish such breastworks and defense overnight must have been the work of 12,000 colonial troops.

The British got out of Boston.

Washington made Putnam full colonel with title — Engineer of the Army.

Later Washington sent for Putnam to organize the fortification of New York City, then West Point, which the colonel suggested as site for a military school.

Still later in the war Putnam wanted the Congress to create a professional army department of engineers. They did not do this, so Putnam withdrew from the Continental Army and joined the Massachusetts line as colonel of a regiment under Gates against Burgoyne. In the spoils of that campaign Putnam appropriated Burgoyne's large camp tent.

Washington continued to call upon him when he needed him for the Continental Army, and General Anthony Wayne chose him for his hand-picked "Wayne Brigade" for assaulting Stony Point.

In late 1782 Putnam, like Washington, wanted to retire to his farm (and his seven children), but Washington could not spare him.

Of all the generals the Pickering group could have chosen to get the Army Plan for the new state to General Washington, and to persuade him to present it to Congress, Rufus Putnam was the one.

The officers invited him to make changes or additions. Putnam liked the plan. However, now wearing authority as easily as an old faded uniform, he did make changes. He added some specifics about the land division including that the six mile township system of surveys be used.

His important action was that he wrote a very strong cover statement summarizing the main advantages of the Pickering Plan to the government:

-retention of the west from the hungry grasp of England, France and Spain by establishing on the western ground an armed population of military personnel;

-establishing financial credit for the bankrupt government by wiping out an enormous chunk of debt by redeeming the bounty land warrants;

-cash income for the government from the increased value of government lands adjacent to the proposed settlement;

-placing an armed cushion of settlement between the Indians and the seaboard population. White man's hair still brought $4.50 delivered at Detroit.

The strength of his letter was his statement that *if the plan were approved he, Putnam, would personally lead a party to colonize a tract.*

Putnam added some signatures to the petition, restyled it *The Newburgh Proposal*, and presented it to Washington.

The general of the armies acted immediately.

(June 17, 1783)

He presented the petition and the proposal to Congress along with Putnam's arguments, June 17, 1783, with his own urgent recommendation that *"the lands described be immediately surveyed and the new state formed quickly."*

Deeply scarred that his comrades in arms were unpaid, the general told Congress that this was *"the most rational and practical scheme which can be adopted by a great proportion of the officers and soldiers of our army."*

However, the Congress was at that very moment embroiled in the squabbling of the states over ownership of the very lands the Pickering Plan wanted for a new state.

Even the authoritative wishes of the great general from Mt. Vernon could not cut through the greed. It was in fact at this hung moment in history a haunting aggravation to congressmen. It demonstrated anew that they did not even have a fingerhold on the formation of a nation. Thirteen separate sovereign nations were willing to jeopardize the whole for their individual pieces of the continent.

It was a new reminder also that the ghost of the unpaid soldiery might rise up and beat all the states to ownership of the west.

Far from E Pluribus Unum, it could become every state for itself, every man for himself.

The Congress gave the petition no action.

With this rejection, troops drifted out of camp. But they carried an angst that would spread. They did not intend to "go starve and be forgotten." Some headed west. With all that unoccupied land available, who would ever find a man if he appropriated a hundred acres?

Congress now knew that while they were trying to resolve the ownership of the west, the people would not wait long, in fact were not waiting. A fairly steady stream of bold and discontent men were threading pack trains and a few wagons through gaps in the Alleghenies into the back country. They were open-minded to accept Indian attack protection from the French, English or Spanish nations, or to start their own.

Some Indian factors and some traders at Ft. Pitt who outfitted parties moving west down the Ohio River estimated there were already 110,000 squatters west of the Alleghenies, operating under no government and wanting none.

A Pittsburgh trader reported counting 600 boats in five years heading downriver carrying 650 wagons; and he had estimated some 9,000 horses had moved through, headed southwest.

The Pickering Plan lay like a dead man's watch, still ticking.

It was clear now to the Congress that if they should be able to settle the ownership of the vast West, they had better have ready for instant use a plan for governing it. Someone in Congress who had the knowledge and the political support to gain passage should be devising that plan — immediately.

But who?

Dayton-Montgomery County Public Library
Thomas Jefferson

Chapter 4: Mr. Jefferson and Mr. Monroe

And Two Stepping Stones To Nationhood

Leaders trusted him with missions that required knowing the mistakes of history's old governments combined with an inventive bent for new ones. Square faced with a square cut helmet of still reddish hair, Thomas Jefferson was a scholar and an inventor.

The Congress appointed him the following fall to head a committee to design quickly an ordinance for disposal and governance of the West.

(October, 1783)

The inventive turn of mind would be needed. He must invent an ordinance which would capture the votes of many hostile congressmen like Richard Spaight and Rufus King, whose constituents felt the West was none of the federal government's business; it belonged to the states. And Jefferson's ordinance must get the votes of others who were so unaware of the rich vastness of "the backland" that they legislated as if the sun set an hour's ride west of Ft. Pitt.

Jefferson knew his Congress.

It was not large, a dozen and a half men, a baker's two dozen on its best days, coming and going as their private affairs required or their funds expired. Six to nine states usually attended, New Hampshire sporadically, Rhode Island seldom, which suited the others as the spoiled child state was always light in the financial pot. Congress diluted its own minimal authority further by moving about — Philadelphia, New York, Princeton. But in one regard it was fixed: the West belonged to the individual states.

Jefferson's 1784 map called for 10 states

The brilliant Jefferson, thus far prominent on western land matters, had as committeemen Chase of Maryland and Howell of Rhode Island.

Politically, Jefferson could count on certain nearly automatic votes. Beyond the respect he commanded from veteran leaders who knew he had risked everything in '76 with the Declaration, a small cult of young hero worshippers had risen to Congress like Monroe and Spaight, who thought Jefferson hung the moon. The committee worked intensively for thirty days, developing the *Ordinance of 1784*.

Ordinance of 1784

It was called the *Jefferson Plan* to lubricate it through Congress. Many of the ideas were Jefferson's, including dividing the backland between the mountains and the Mississippi into ten states: Sylvania - Saratoga - Michigania - Washington - Cheronesus - Polypotamia - Assenisipia - Pelisipia - Illinoia - Mesopotamia, to be located as shown.

The very comprehensive plan provided for admission of these territories to full statehood in stages as their populations rose to certain levels. It decreed that each would adopt a constitution from one of the old states.

To relax those congressmen who feared the rising possibility that new states would break off and join Spain or France or form separate nations, Jefferson's ordinance stipulated, *"shall remain forever part of the United States."*

To allay fears that such new states could grow into unruly monsters, overpowering the parent, the committee wrote in, *"subject to government by Congress and the Articles of Confederation."*

The Jefferson committee, primarily concerned with the land, nevertheless worked on the philosophical and political aspects of future settlement, trying to avoid the pitfalls of Europe, declaring for example, the new states *"shall admit no hereditary titled person."* There were to be no dukes in the back country.

Well known to most congressmen was Jefferson's desire, along with many other slave-holding southern leaders, to eliminate slavery.

Ten vigorous southern abolitionist societies were active. Jefferson wrote into the ordinance forbiddance of slavery in new states. Politically he softened that by adding *"after 1800."* Why Jefferson thought slavery with a 16-year foothold could be cut off at midnight December 31, 1799 is puzzling.

By February 21st the committee was satisfied enough with its Ordinance of 1784 to present it to Congress in committee of the whole.

(March 17, 1784) Congress rejected it and assigned it back to committee on March 17th to be reworked. The ordinance was too complete for passage. Its profound merits were veiled under a clutter of highly specific trivia.

For example the names Pelisipia, Assenisipia and Polypotamia were too Mediterranean on the tongue for some. The arbitrary specification of exact boundaries started arguments which hid the benefit. Georgia and the huge Carolinas aggressively opposed carving their enormous backlands into more states.

The committee reworked the ordinance. They substituted numbers for the state names and loosened proposed boundaries slightly. The proposed new states south of the Ohio River were only implied in dotted line, leaving the deep southerners negotiating room. North of the Ohio River the committee diagramed only six states, the future Ohio appearing only as a sliver.

(March 22, 1784) Jefferson presented this less provocative ordinance. Some further revisions were argued into it on the floor. The committee redrafted, bringing the ordinance again before Congress for approval on April 19th.

At this point, 26-year-old Richard D. Spaight rose to be heard in a deep-timbered drawl. The Spaights had been ruling part of North Carolina over a century and were accustomed to telling newcomers the rules. Although he was a devoted Jefferson follower, Spaight moved the antislavery article stricken. The president of Congress at that moment was Howell, of Jefferson's own committee. But he could not deny Spaight's call.

The *timing* of calling for a vote was exploited regularly as a strategy because a congressman could survey at a glance the very

44

small number in attendance and judge quite accurately the hour when his proposal had best chance to pass.

The voting system did not register the individual votes, only a state's aye or nay, the individual delegate's votes having determined that. A tie within a state delegation was a nay for the state. Thus a proposal could win a majority of individual votes and still lose.

Howell gaveled for order and phrased the question, "Shall the words moved to be stricken stand? Massachusetts. Mr. Gerry?"

Massachusetts - Gerry, aye; Partridge, aye; the state, aye.
Rhode Island - Ellery, aye; Howell, aye; the state, aye.
New York - DeWitt, aye; Paine, aye; the state, aye.
New Jersey - Dick, aye; only one vote.
Pennsylvania - Hand, aye; Stone, aye; the state, aye.
Maryland - McHenry, aye; Stone, aye; the state, aye.
Virginia - Jefferson, aye; Stone, aye, Hardy, nay; Mercer, nay; the state, nay.
North Carolina - Williamson, aye; Spaight, nay; the state, nay.
South Carolina - Reed, nay; Beresford, nay; the state, nay.

Even though over twice as many voted to retain, the clause was stricken (the necessary number of states, then seven, did not vote to retain).

The again revised ordinance came up for third reading.

The item against hereditary titles was removed. Added was a prohibition against new states taxing federal lands within their borders, and against taxing absentee land owners more than residents.

On this day the Jefferson Ordinance, became the law of the land. (April 23, 1784)

To activate it there was under preparation by another Jefferson committee an ordinance for the future disposal of those lands not yet ceded to the government by the states. However, when presented to Congress, it was defeated, six states voting nay.

Pickering later wrote to vigorous abolitionist Congressman Rufus King asking him to get the antislavery clause back into the Ordinance of 1784. King, a burly young statehouse veteran from Massachusetts, was a power figure in Congress, gaining his way by alternating charm and blunt rudeness.

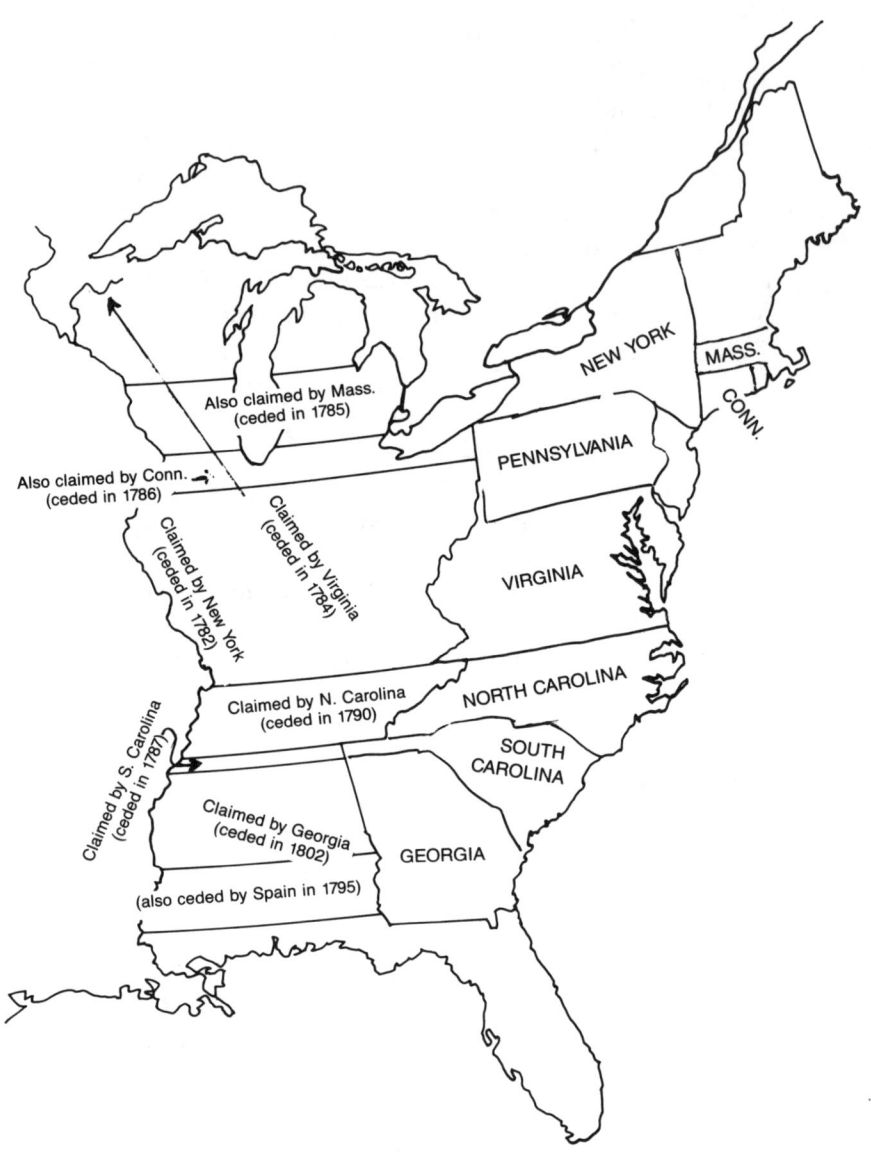

Conflicting land claims stalled settlement

In the high-pitched voice so startling in the stout, authoritarian body, King moved:

"Resolved that there shall be neither slavery nor involuntary servitude in any of the States described (...) and this shall be an article of compact and (...) fundamental principle of the constitution of the 13 original states, and each of the states described in said resolve (...)"

This was referred to committee. They softened it by adding the fugitive slave provision. New free states could not prevent pursuit and recapture by slave owners from the old states. The committee proposed the provision be effective in 1801. However, this change never made it back to the floor before some other events interfered.

Frustrating every effort to plan for the West was the knowledge that the Confederation did not clearly own it. The states would not give it up.

The High Road

There are different blends of patriotism, some with a higher content of materialism or altruism or ego or commercialism.

The Virginia blend went right to the root of the word — pater. They were fathers. With the authority and noblesse of fathers, they would judge and discipline the national population and make the people do what was good for them. Also like fathers, they would give up their best loved possessions for their young.

Virginia leaders loved land, thousands of acres of it. A Yankee side hill farm to a Virginian was a kitchen garden. If a Virginia leader did not own a township or two, he was embarrassed. Washington himself hungrily acquired thousands of acres even while struggling to pay his bills.

Virginia's claim to the West was the giant claim. Her original south line cut due west "from sea to sea." Her original north border slanted northwest encompassing the entire Northwest Territory, prevented from reaching the Arctic by Britain's new boundary in the Great Lakes.

But outranking Virginia's love of her land was her concern for uniting the states under an effective national government. Virginia, therefore, led the states in giving up western land claims. On September 6, 1780 the Congress, led by the Virginians, recommended the states make liberal land cessions.

On the second day of January 1781 Virginia yielded "all right, title and claim (...) to the territory northwest of the river Ohio," subject to certain conditions. She wanted to reserve lands to honor her bounty land warrants to her veterans. She wanted to be repaid for George Rogers Clark's expenses in conquering British posts in the territory and she wanted land to recompense Clark and his soldiers for the Kaskaskia campaign.

While it is true that New York offered to cede lands in late 1780, she did not formally cede until March 1, 1781. However, she had only a small southwest corner of New York to cede, and that on a vague basis of her guardianship over the Iroquois, who in turn, claimed the West.

(March 1, 1784)

Over Virginia's cession, however, began a long and bitter argument against *accepting* her conditions. Finally, on September 13, 1783, Congress adopted a court report granting Virginia *some* of her requests. Virginia agreed to this on December 29, 1783. On March 1, 1784 Virginia delivered the deed, signed by Jefferson, Hardy, Monroe and Arthur Lee.

With that done, Virginia leaders pressured the other states.

Massachusetts would cede in 1785 after negotiations with New York. Connecticut would yield in 1786, with reservations.

The Carolinas and Georgia continued to hold out.

The 1784 Ordinance was law, but toothless because, even with Virginia's huge cession, part of the ownership of the west was still uncertain. The ordinance was also limp because it did not crisply enough define the governance of the new states. It did not contain incentives for settlers.

Another Attempt

Just after passage of the Ordinance of 1784, Jefferson was needed

48

in France with John Adams to represent the young American con- (May 1784) federation in final trade and peace negotiatons.

Moving into Jefferson's shoes now on the subject of western land governance came a man 15 years younger, James Monroe.

How effective could a 27-year-old youngster be in the wake of such national giants as Jefferson, Chase and Howell?

Monroe gave many seniors a start when he first walked into Congress because of the stunning likeness to a younger Washington. Although a much handsomer man, Monroe had a nearly identical patrician profile, the same commanding bearing, and despite his youth, the same winkless grey-blue eyes which listened without comment.

He had dropped out of William and Mary College at 18 for the war and had smelled the smoke and death at Harlem Heights, White Plains, Trenton, Monmouth, Germantown and Brandywine.

The only mark of youth not calloused over was his admiration of his law teacher, Thomas Jefferson, whom he would follow, though not blindly, for years.

In preparing to create a sharper ordinance, Monroe twice rode west to see for himself the territory northwest of the Ohio River. He concluded that Jefferson's ten straight ruler line boundaries were unnatural.

They made no accommodation of the land's curving shapes — rivers, lakes, mountains and plains. They cut the region into too many states, too small. They deprived some future states of a fair share of natural advantages.

There was also new urgency to establish a more specific governance policy for the West because pressure for cession of land by the states to the confederation was promising.

Monroe's committee members, largely senior to him in experience or stature, were William S. Johnson of Connecticut; John Kean of South Carolina; domineering Rufus King of Massachusetts, outspoken in lack of affection for the West; and the rising statesman, Charles Pinckney of South Carolina. However they accepted Monroe's leadership. Even John Quincy Adams, critical of everyone but God, recognized Monroe as a strong future leader.

This committee began hammering out a new law, "An Ordinance for Ascertaining the Mode of Disposing of Lands in the Western Territory." The short name was the *Ordinance of 1785*.

The Ordinance of 1785

This new committee was in for a rocky voyage.

Their early draft had really important improvements. It provided for township surveys and for land sales in *small* lots. Why important? That meant the small farmer could get in. If only large tracts were sold, large investors would buy huge tracts and hold for price rise. The western forests would remain vacant of Americans, defeating settlement.

Next, Monroe's committee laid a highly specific and workable diagram leading from territorial government to full statehood.

Suddenly, before the ordinance was approved by Congress, Monroe quit the committee to start a law practice in Fredericksburg. Johnson moved to chairman. King and Kean were so much absent that new men were assigned: Melancthon Smith of New York, John Henry of Maryland and Nathan Dane of Massachusetts. Dane, a young lawyer with knife-edged vertical features and equally sharp mind, was a dedicated lay churchman who carried into committee a taut and punishing religion. He would become important.

Dane largely did the drafting of this Ordinance of 1785, assisted by Pinckney on the parts concerning government. They made changes from the original Monroe document. A territory could apply for statehood when its population reached 1/13th of the population of the original 13 states.

Dane inserted an important innovation. In case a man died without a will his estate would be inherited not only by the eldest son, but by all his children equally, male and female.

From the previous draft of the Ordinance of 1785 the rights of habeas corpus and trial by jury of peers were retained.

It was a good document, but it was in for trouble from the rest of the Congress, forcing several revisions. Congress found it too generous to the territory, allowing too much autonomy. They demanded more federal control, for example, when the territory had 5000 free males, the settlers could elect one representative to a territorial legislature for every 500, but Congress would *appoint* five.

This Ordinance of 1785 would be in so much trouble that it would not be finally passed until 1786.

However, strangely enough, Congress would put one part of it into action in early 1785, even before passage.

Outlaw squatters were widening the wheel ruts into the Northwest Territory, riling the Shawnees, Delawares and Wyandots. Congress persuaded three states to furnish militia. Col. Harmar sent 100 men to establish Ft. Harmar at the Muskingum and Ohio River confluence to turn back intruders.

But they could not stem the flow. It was therefore imperative to survey the land so that these immigrants could *buy* land, before they stole it.

The Seven Ranges

The Ordinance of 1785 did specifically mandate surveying into townships one large triangle cupped in the northwest shore of the Ohio River southwest of Pennsylvania — the Seven Ranges Survey.

This would be the first application in the world of the township, or rectangular plan of dividing the land as ordered in the Ordinance of 1785.

Land management had always been a battleground of snake-shaped contestable boundaries in which corner markers dried up, washed away or burned down. This new system would let the young republic manage, price and sell its vast lands in standard packages. Boundaries could be re-established from surveyors' notes despite fires, floods and lawyers.

Those particular seven ranges were not at this time themselves important to this story. What made them a turning point was the requirement that they *immediately* be surveyed. This forced a survey team to go into the Ohio Country. That in turn brought on stage *one particular individual* who would reignite fading dreams of the aging war veterans who had given up on the Pickering Plan and nearly forgotten where they had stored their yellowing military warrants for bounty lands.

While the rest of the Ordinance of 1785 would not be applied enough to make it much more than a practice run, the Seven Ranges Survey alone made it strangely crucial to the America story.

Chapter 5: Tupper

Ever wonder why on state and county roads west of the Appalachians all the way to the Coast, country cross roads have a little corner stone marked something like "R 7 Twp 6"? And why, west of the Appalachians, our counties and towns and farms are almost precisely square? And it is usually exactly three miles from the town limits to the center of town if you're moving north-south or east-west?

The Ordinance of 1785 triggered the appointment of one surveyor from each state for the Seven Ranges survey. To protect the surveyors from increasingly agitated Indians, a garrison of 100 was in place at Pennsylvania's Ft. McIntosh at the mouth of Beaver Creek north of Ft. Pitt.

These surveyors were to mark off a piece of the Ohio country into seven north-south ranges each six miles wide, then divide these into townships six miles square. The townships would later be surveyed into 36 sections, each a mile square (640 acres).

The surveyors would blaze their marks on trees, but also note the chains and rods in their journals so that if the trees were felled, blown down or burned, the lines on the land could be recreated out of court for centuries hence.

One surveyor from each state was specified so that each might return to his own state and describe the lands to its citizens. Rufus Putnam was named from Massachusetts to the survey. However, he was in the middle of a contract from Massachusetts to survey ten

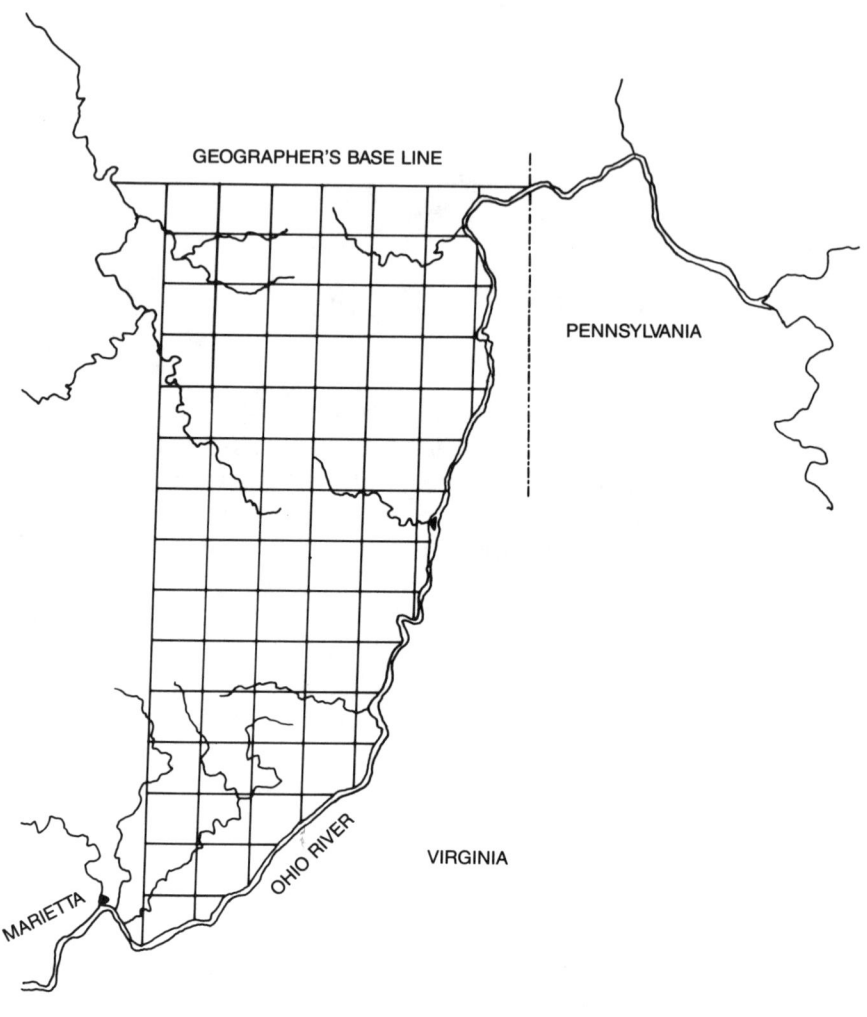

Map of the Seven Ranges Survey; each six-mile range was divided into townships six miles square

townships in its "province of Mayne." He recommended to Thomas Hutchins, the national geographer, that his place be taken by a long-time friend, like a brother to him, Colonel Benjamin Tupper.

Tupper, exactly the same age as Putnam, was also born and raised in Massachusetts. Tupper's father also died when Ben was a boy. Tupper also enlisted as a private with the British in the French and Indian War, and then also enlisted early in the Revolution. Like Putnam he saw heavy action and rose in the ranks. Like Putnam he also became a skilled surveyor, very important at this moment in history. He was tuned to the wild and knew something of the region he would now survey.

Under National Geographer Thomas Hutchins, Tupper reported for launching the Seven Ranges Survey in the fall of 1785. Of the 13 surveyors, only eight arrived. Captain Hutchins, with his eight deputy surveyors, 30 chain men, ax-men and pack-horse handlers, moved out of Ft. Pitt to run these first official American national township lines, the Seven Ranges. The ranges were to be numbered serially west from the Ohio River where it turns to flow south southwesterly.

On September 22, 1785 they began running their base line west perpendicular to the west boundary of Pennsylvania. The teams trudged and scrambled over forested ridges and through swamps and blowdowns, blazing their marks on witness trees. They recorded these and noted in their journals the soil conditions, streams, mill sites, salt licks, species of hardwoods.

One young man on Tupper's team was his own son, Anselm, learning the surveying profession from a master.

However, in the velvet darkness the teams began hearing noises too heavy for small game and too light for moose. And in the wet light of mornings some horses were missing. Surveyors became aware that they were being shadowed in the woods by earlier Americans of Shawnee descent who saw the marks on the trees and knew the white men were drawing lines on the land which could become fences. They let the white men advance into the Ohio Country along Hutchins' base line until they were well beyond easy support of Ft. McIntosh.

36	30	24	18	12	6
35	29	23	17	11	5
34	28	22	16	10	4
33	27	21	15	9	3
32	26	20	14	8	2
31	25	19	13	7	1

Six-mile-square township had 36 one-square-mile sections

Then they struck.

Hutchins pulled back to the Ohio River. He sought out the friendly Delaware chief, Captain Pipe, asking his protection for the surveyors against the Shawnees. Pipe shook his head.

Hutchins discharged his laborers in order to seek military support. The troops at Ft. McIntosh were no longer available. They were suddenly needed downstream at Ft. Finney to protect Americans there trying to repair the Treaty of Ft. McIntosh by right of which these surveyors were on these ceded lands.

The Shawnees, however, claimed those previous Indian cessions at Ft. McIntosh were made by chiefs not authorized to bargain away these Indian lands. The survey was delayed while General Parsons and other U.S. agents were dispatched again to attempt to clear Indian titles in meetings on the Great Miami River.

During the delay, Benjamin Tupper detached himself from the survey to explore into the Seven Ranges region. And he received reports from men coming back out of the wilderness to Ft. Pitt. These reports corroborated what he already believed about the upper

Ohio Valley — good hardwood timber on the hills, lowlands well veined with streams to dampen dark loam a foot and a half deep that crumbled nicely in the fist. In the few openings in the hardwood cover there were grasses stemmed thick as a man's small finger promising three grazings per summer.

To a Massachusetts man who had removed rocks from sidehills to clear pasture, this was exciting news.

In the month when the bucks lose their horns, other surveyors brought Tupper evidence that game was plentiful.

To Tupper, this called for action.

Destiny's Meeting

Since the delay in the survey continued, it became possible for Tupper to leave the field. A tall, rugged man, on the heavy side, he packed saddlebags in November 1785 for a hard five-week ride. He rode east across Pennsylvania, across New York and up into Massachusetts to the top of the high ridge between the Connecticut and Merrimac Rivers to the town of Rutland. He rode out to the eastern outskirts of the town to a large square classic house where lived the man who was now the heart and spirit of this hundred-year-old town — Rufus Putnam. Tupper reached there January 9, 1786.

He was welcomed prodigiously by his old friend, but he only waited for the mount to be grained to get to his mission...to explain to Putnam the proof of what they had both long suspected about the merits of the Ohio Valley in the southeastern part of the Ohio Country just west of Pennsylvania's back country.

(January 9, 1786)

In Putnam's house, warmed by the fire and distilled grain waters, the two began an historic conversation that would last all night.

It ended with a proposition pivotal to North American history.

Putnam may well have been among the hundred living men in America who best grasped the actual shape and texture of the lands east of the Mississippi between the St. Lawrence and the Gulf of Mexico. He had covered much of it during the Revolution, and had heard much about the Ohio Valley from General Washington who loved that region and owned land there. And he had seen some of the deep south when seeking land promised him by the British for his service in the Seven Years War.

Putnam told Tupper his impression of the lands he was surveying in Maine from a farmer's viewpoint "is not fit for cultivation and (...) with the climate a man ought to consider himself curst even in this world who is doomed to inhabit there as a cultivator of the lands only."

Against that, Tupper reported that the Ohio Country lands "are of a much better quality than any other known to the New England people; the climate, seasons, products (...) are in fact equal to the most flattering accounts that have been published of them."

Combining their knowledge before the fire in the house in Rutland, the two men determined to found a new colony in the Ohio Country.

(January 10, 1786)
When dawn lit the east slope of Rutland on January 10, 1786, Putnam and Tupper had a plan to announce. In several Massachusetts journals they published "An Information:"

"The subscribers take this method to inform all officers and soldiers who have served in the late War, and who are (...) to receive certain tracts of land in the Ohio Country; and also other good citizens who wish to become adventurers in that delightful region; that from personal inspection, together with other incontestable evidences, they are fully satisfied that the lands in that quarter are..."

The document spent the next 35 words, worthy of the best modern land promoters, proving that it was a "delightful region;" then announced their intention to move west and start a settlement there, using bounty land warrants to pay for the land. They stated their proposition:

"That an association by the name of the OHIO COMPANY be formed of all such as wish to become purchasers, &c., in that Country (who reside in the Commonwealth of Massachusetts only, or to extend to the inhabitants of other states as shall be agreed on)."

The Information then proposed that all who were interested should:

"...meet in their respective counties (...) at ten o'clock a.m., on Wednesday the fifth day of February next, and that each county or meeting there assembled, chuse a delegate or delegates, to meet at the *Bunch of Grapes Tavern* in Boston, on Wednesday the first day of March next at ten o'clock a.m., then and there to determine upon a General Plan of association for said Company (...)."

To insure workability, as military men would, they then prescribed exactly where and when (February 15th) the interested parties from each county should meet:

"Those of Suffolk County at the *Bunch of Grapes* in Boston—Essex at Capt. Webb's in Salem—Hampshire at Pomeroy's in North Hampton—Plymouth at Bartlett's in Plymo—Barnstable, Dukes & Nantucket Counties, at Howland's in Barnstable — Bristol at Crokers in Taunton—York at Woodbridge's in York—Worster at Patch's in Worster—Cumberland and Lincoln at Shattuck's in Falmouth—Berkshire at Dibble's in Lennox.
Rufus Putnam
Benjamin Tupper"

Those were trustworthy signatures to Massachusetts war veterans. The message was the first good news many veteran bounty land warrant holders had heard since demobilization — a chance for those who had retained their bounty land warrants or final certificates. Men searched old trunks for their bounty warrants.

The Bunch of Grapes Headquarters

On the first day of March seven men tied horses outside the Bunch of Grapes and went in to look for Putnam and Tupper. In from

(March 1, 1786)

Suffolk County walked John Mills and the aggressive Major Winthrop Sargent. From Middlesex County where the Revolution had begun at Concord came John Brooks and Thomas Cushing. From Barnstable County, Abraham Williams. Two came from Berkshire County, John Patterson and Johlaliel Woodbridge. From historic Plymouth County, Crocker Sampson walked in. Putnam was from Worcester County, Tupper from Hampshire.

From Essex County came one of New England's most distinguished men, relaxed and genial Manasseh Cutler.

Wherever they may have begun life...on farms or even as an indentured apprentice...these were by now experienced men with gray in the hair. Several had soldiered under two flags and risen to field grade rank and having lost much in the Revolution, were nevertheless surviving successfully in civilian work. Therefore the organization meeting proceeded quite professionally.

Putnam was elected chairman, Sargent clerk.

Tupper described the region.

Putnam, Cutler, Col. Brooks, Capt. Cushing and Major Sargent were appointed to draw up articles of association. The delegates would stay over a day while this was being done.

(March 3, 1786 3:30 pm)

On March 3 the delegates reassembled at half after 3:00 o'clock to listen to the articles, lengthy and comprehensive, providing for many contingencies which these experienced veterans could foresee.

In summary the articles proposed that this Ohio Company would raise no more than a million dollars "for the sole purpose and entire use of purchasing the land from the government."

Each share would be $1000. A shareholder could use his bounty land warrant(s) for this. Each shareholder would contribute, in addition to one year's interest on the certificate, $10 in hard money for an expense fund. No one could own more than five shares.

The group would allow one year to sign up the additional shareholders and would reconvene March 8, 1787 in Boston, hoping to have signed up a thousand shares.

(March 8, 1787)

But on March 8th the following year, when they reconvened at Bracket's Tavern, Boston, only 250 shares had been subscribed.

Why so few?

The objection encountered was that under the Ordinance of 1785, they could not secure one large compact piece of land. That ordinance, remember, to prevent speculators locking up large tracts, limited the single purchase, and further provided that the federal government retain alternate sections and that bounty land warrants would *only* be accepted for alternate sections. However, the organizers felt this could be overcome by negotiation. Therefore, after electing directors, Putnam, Cutler and Parsons, they appointed General Parsons, of Middletown, Connecticut, to travel to the Congress in New York and negotiate purchase of the land as one individual tract.

General Parsons made the Ohio Company's land purchase proposal to Congress. While the proposition was received cordially enough, there were only two days remaining before many congressional delegates were planning to go home for recess. Two days was not enough time for any congress to act on such a proposal, let alone this particular Congress, powerless and divided. (May 8-9, 1787)

There would not be a quorum present until July 4th. Therefore General Parsons came back to report this to Putnam and leave him a copy of a map of the tract of land he proposed to the Congress for the Ohio Company purchase on the Scioto River in the Ohio country. He then returned to his home.

Putnam, thinking over what he had heard from Parsons, and studying the map and conferring with Tupper, was disappointed in the piece of land for which Parsons was dealing. It was too westerly. Putnam was convinced that the land astride the Muskingum east of the Scioto was better, and safer from Indian attack.

He dispatched a message to Major Sargent, then in New York, to stop Congress from any action on The Ohio Company proposal as they could not consent to Parson's choice of land. There would be a new purchase proposal forthcoming.

Putnam could not personally go to New York to the Congress because of the completion date required by his Maine survey contract with Massachusetts.

He then made a pivotal decision. He selected Manasseh Cutler to go to Congress and take charge of negotiations.

Cutler's was a double assignment. First he must persuade the

Congress to pass legislation for the governance of the western territory which would be acceptable to the men in The Ohio Company. It must assure them that they ultimately could become a new state in the Union with the same and equal status as the other states and with full representation.

Second, Cutler must get Congressional approval of the details of The Ohio Company's purchase proposal including the number of acres, the location, the price, the payment plan, and that the Company own *all* the acres, not alternate sections.

This mission must necessarily be considered impossible when one looks at the record. For eight years the Congress had not been able even to agree on a system of governance for the West. The Congress was so opposed to the formation of a new state and so cool to the favoring of war veterans that even the urgent advocacy by the most respected commander-in-chief of the Continental Army for the Pickering Plan was ignored.

Why expect this effort to succeed?

As for gaining approval of The Ohio Company purchase terms, the Company had not even yet assembled the million dollars, having signed only 250 subscribers. They were asking to buy for under a dollar an acre, considering the market value of bounty land warrants. For this small price they wanted the entire machinery of government to be established and paid for by the national government at a time when the states did not want a central government and paid taxes only at their pleasure, Rhode Island and New Hampshire declining even that.

Additionally, the most active men in Congress were from Georgia, the Carolinas, Virginia and Maryland. And this proposal was to come from a Yankee who was not even a combat veteran. And if a new state should result from The Ohio Company proposal it would be another Yankee state at a time when there were too many of those already, according to southern congressmen like Richard Spaight of Carolina.

How could Putnam lay such a charge on Cutler?

However, before going to New York with Cutler, it is important to note an enormous conspiracy in Philadelphia.

Chapter 6: The General

And The Philadelphia Conspiracy

Will the General be there?

Wherever American leadership met in late 1786 or early 1787 in Williamsburg, Fredericksburg, Richmond, Philadelphia, New York, Hartford and Boston that question centered the gossip.

At that time, when they said the General, they didn't need to say his name. While the grand, flamboyant generals who had been so much more qualified, more articulate, more forward, more ambitious receded largely into commerce and autobiography, the stature of the stoic Virginia planter rose, a colossus here and abroad. Perspective revealed the enormity of his accomplishment and his leadership.

The pressure upon the General to attend the great conspiracy scheduled for Philadelphia built from all directions. And, as with many of his decisions, it wrenched him nights worse than the rheumatism and ague which also fostered his indecision. If he traveled to Philadelphia in May of 1787, would ill health render him ineffective in the middle of this critical conspiracy? (May 2, 1787)

Late in 1786 the General formally notified the Virginia House of Delegates that he would not be a delegate to the Federal Convention in Philadelphia. Ill health, he wrote.

The pressure persisted. The General resisted. He had always guarded his credibility; and his attendance at the Philadelphia convention, he pointed out, would be in conflict with his final address to the state governors at the close of the war, "I give a last farewell to the cares of office and all the employments of public life."

As spring approached the pressure on the General to attend increased, particularly from the Virginia legislature. He explained to Jemmy Madison that he had already sent notice to the officers of the Society of the Cincinnati (the fraternity of retired army officers) that he could not preside over their triennial reunion in Philadelphia because of health* and would not accept reelection as Society president.

Therefore, "I could not appear at the same time and place (...) without giving offense to the Society." Washington's loyalty and love for these fellow officers was profound (even though he fought their political ambitions).

James Madison persisted, explaining that the General's absence at Philadelphia "might defeat the whole scheme."

The Scheme

The scheme, history's greatest conspiracy, by far, was to create a nation, the United States of America, by constitution.
Did we not have that?
Far from it.
The states would not hear of it.
The words national or nation were fighting words.
Confederation was bad enough, but acceptable, if the Confederation were kept powerless. The thought of a constitution was intolerable. Thirteen sovereignties had no intention of being joined and ruled by a constitution. Articles of Confederation were acceptable only so long as they remained merely a commercial treaty of neighborly trade accommodations with no power to tax, raise armies, or coerce.

However, here and there in every city were handfuls of history-schooled men, some educated in Europe, who knew from Rome

---

*He had other reasons. Many members wanted the Society to become a military elite with political power. Washington fought this concept.

forward what happens to new close-neighboring nations. They knew from books what Washington knew from the lingering British-Indian presence in Great Lakes forts, "I do not conceive we can exist long as a nation without having lodged somewhere a power, which will pervade the whole union."

The "power" they wanted to establish was a national government with a constitution.

The headless Congress with its voluntary revolving lazy susan membership was powerless to tax, to enforce law, or raise arms. The annual income of the treasury undershot one third of the interest on the debts.

Groups of two and three states were proposing to ally themselves as nations; civil war was very probable without a binding constitution. With Shays' Rebellion, Washington's optimism in the reasonableness of common men temporarily deserted him, "...that mankind when left to themselves are unfit for their own government."

He had great leadership hopes for a protege, young James Madison. He warned Jemmy to work for national government, "Thirteen sovereignties pulling against each other (...) will soon bring ruin on the whole."

But there was no way the states would accept a convention to create a constitution.

A Code Phrase And A Tacit Understanding

A conspiracy of nationalist leaders, however, recognized an innocuous spark and fanned it.

A small caterrumpus bubbled up on the Virginia-Maryland border over common use of the Potomac River. Commissioners from both states met at Mt. Vernon in March, 1785 to cool the heartburn. Out of it came a resolve to meet once a year about these commercial problems. Maryland decided to invite Delaware and Pennsylvania next time. Virginia simultaneously proposed a meeting of all states only "to consider (...) commercial regulations."

This in turn led to the Annapolis Convention, again only to resolve trade arguments. Only five of the 13 states sent delegates;

but amazingly — out of that meeting came a call for "a foedaral convention" of all states "to render (...) the foederal government adequate to the exigencies of the union."

Again, the deliberate implication was that strictly commercial relations would be advanced. They wanted to give the impression that they were merely going to patch the roof on the aging Articles of Confederation.

But those who engineered the meeting hoped to put in a new foundation — a constitution, designing a national government. "Foederal Convention" to the activists was a password for constitutional convention.

Congress Hated Convention

Congress hated the idea of the convention. However, the competition of this new federal convention threatened to further weaken the Congress' feeble stature unless it preserved its authority by itself calling the convention. Congress did this, but specifically limited the function, "for the sole and express purpose of revising the Articles of Confederation and reporting to Congress (...) such alterations and provisions."

The schemers, with far larger ideas, carefully avoided the words national and constitution.

Those pressing Washington to attend argued that the mere rumor that he rejected the appointment would cause other states to send lesser men as delegates, guaranteeing failure. Some states might send none.

Others advised the General that he was the only one who could command discipline among delegates of feuding states.

Still others told him that if he declined, the resulting constitution would fail of ratification by the populace because "Washington wasn't there."

The General was bombarded with these latter arguments by the leaders in Virginia, Massachusetts and New York...Madison, Monroe, Randolph and Hamilton, most insistent.

The nucleus of nationalists bullied other states into sending their most distinguished men by explaining the General's reluctance to attend a feeble convention of less than first rank leaders.

The mail bags at Mt. Vernon arrived full of requests that Washington attend. Martha Washington, with two grandchildren present, viewed the bags sadly. She had been sure "we would have been left to a peaceful old age together."

A few wise men began counseling Washington not to go, at least at first.

General Knox, his loyalty still hard as steel after his body had gone to suet, pointed out that, should the General be involved, and the conference fail to produce a government, Washington's great prestige would be smashed. Then it would be unavailable to shore up the union. Washington should be held in reserve as the last resource.

Martha Washington worried about what such a pivotal meeting would do to the General's health; but she was prepared for the price. However, the chief debate went on inside Washington's own heart and mind.

First he did not want to leave the farm where, despite rheumatic pain, he was in the most content period of his life, riding over the acres, starting projects he would never finish, buying land he would never see.

Second, he had an action man's resignation about any convention of talkers. Third, he feared that if few delegates, and lesser persons at that, arrived in convention that negative showing would foredoom failure and hasten explosion of the union. Fourth, he feared delegates might arrive, he wrote Governor Randolph, "so fettered" by instruction from home that "the great object would be unobtainable."

Friends Advise Staying Away

Some of his closest friends wished him to stay away. His long-time friend, David Humphreys, with whom he was as relaxed as with Knox, urged him to stay away, knowing that if the convention were a failure, Washington, the most conspicuous delegate, would have the farthest to fall.

(April 9, 1787)

John Jay, the attorney, did not want Washington involved because the convention, being called contrary to the amending proviso in the Articles, was illegal. Madison changed his own opinion, telling Washington he ought not appear early. If the opening session forecast failure, he ought not appear at all.

Finally as May drew near, trusted General Knox counseled him, "It is the general wish that you should attend."

By candlelight on the morning of May 9, 1787 the General nodded to his coachman. Thunder grumbled over him four days as he once again reluctantly traveled north to lay everything on the line.

"God Only Knows...What The Result Will Be"

It was like his arrival after Yorktown. Philadelphia's City Light Horse escorted him into crowd-lined streets. Artillery saluted.

Then, when the bells of Philadelphia stopped ringing, the General's fears seemed ratified. On May 14th, the official opening day, so few of 74 pledged delegates arrived that the convention was not called. Virginia was there and Pennsylvania and Rufus King of Massachusetts. The latter was so humiliated that he wrote home to expedite the other delegates.

Delegates straggled in so slowly that each day the convention was postponed again.

But what delegates!

With Washington attending, the states sent their very best. They were young, but experienced and brilliant — the Morrises, Robert and Gouverneur, financial commissioners of the war; the distinguished Virginians, Wythe, Blair, Randolph and Mason; Hamilton of New York; 81-year-old Dr. Ben Franklin; Rutledge and the Pinckneys of South Carolina; Dickinson of Delaware.

They totalled only 55, but they were names which would become the presidents, governors, secretaries of state, and senators for decades to come. Because they were so young in 1787, more public service lay ahead for most of them — Jonathan Dayton of New Jersey 26, Charles Pinckney 29, Hamilton 30. Small statured, quiet, intellectual James (Jemmy) Madison who would be the mastermind might well be called, except for Franklin, the "father" of the convention at an elderly 36.

Two great ones were absent. John Adams and Tom Jefferson were in Europe on American trade and treaty business. In Paris Jefferson received the roster and exclaimed, "an assembly of demi-gods."

Finally, not waiting for the others, they opened the convention near the end of May with only 29 delegates. They elected Washington convention president. For the second time the huge responsibility to create the United States was forced upon him. (Some suspected there would be still a third time he would be called.)

There were a dozen moves which could be said to have saved the convention from disaster, but the second, after sending the finest delegates, was electing Washington president.

As in the Revolution, he found himself in charge of more schooled, brilliant, articulate, flamboyant, experienced men. But in the anger and insufferable heat which lay ahead, it was the winkless cold grey eye of the General upon rebellious delegates which held them sternly to the work six hours a day for four and a half months despite the deep schisms, scheming alliances, stupefying heat and blue bottle flies.

He spoke seldom, but he set the level for the work at its opening: "It is too probable that no plan we propose will be adopted. Perhaps another dreadful conflict is to be sustained. If, to please the people, we offer what we ourselves disapprove, how can we afterwards defend the work? Let us raise a standard to which the wise and honest can repair; the event is in the hands of God."

The message reached the men.

Even the jovial, witty Gouverneur Morris turned very sober saying that he felt he was (Madison noted it in his journal) "a representative of the whole human race, for the whole human race will be affected by the proceedings of this Convention." He asked the men to lift their views above the present and beyond the narrowing limits "from which we derive our political origin." Nevertheless June found them deadlocked.

The delegates made a rule to keep proceedings secret. Tacitly most knew that what they were creating here went far beyond revising the Articles of Confederation. They were creating a nation by creating a national government via a constitution. They knew that if proceedings were not secret, and if the issues began being debated in the streets and taverns, or influenced by lobbyists, they would never succeed. It would be difficult enough inside the hall.

Washington had hoped to conclude quickly. But despite the lofty intent of the delegates in the breezeless, humid hall they were at odds on nearly every plan of government. The large states fought the small; certain states resisted creating a national authority. The issue of varying representation in the government by various sized states was an enormous block. And why should a national government be empowered to veto actions by the states?

Yet in the heat of the nights, men worried about the republic. They continued the arguments over in City Tavern reminding each other, however, the discussions were still secret.

Washington wrote home for more clothes, "I see no end to my staying here."

The subject of this volume is not the Constitutional Convention, except as it relates to the Congress meeting just across New Jersey in the second story of the New York city hall, battling the very same subject impasse.

As Philadelphia seemed hopelessly bogged down, Hamilton went home to New York, angry. Washington's disappointment and disgust grew. He dispatched a note to young Hamilton, "I almost despair of seeing a favorable issue to the proceedings (...) and do therefore repent having any agency in this business."

However, the caged eagle remained on the dais laconically governing the traffic in ideas by brilliant delegates.

Dr. Cutler Packs

Meanwhile up in Massachusetts, The Ohio Company of Associates wanted to begin a new settlement in a large tract north and west of the Ohio River which they could be assured would one day become a state, equal to the original 13.

However, in Philadelphia a powerful contingent favored handling the back lands as Gouverneur Morris advocated, "govern them as provinces, and allow them no voice in our councils."

New England's own Elbridge Gerry opposed the West, believing "...we will create a formidable competitor."

Dr. Cutler, of Ipswich, Massachusetts, knew Gerry's position. He knew Rufus King's bad tempered attitude. But he packed a small trunk for New York. He did not plan to be there long; but for the mission ahead, he would need visiting clothes.

Dayton-Montgomery County Public Library
Manasseh Cutler

Chapter 7: Cutler

July 1787 came on so hot it became an actor in the America story, affecting the work ways of the men closing forever the Congress in New York, and those opening the Constitutional Convention in Philadelphia. Heat rising visibly off the cobblestones and the waters of Philadelphia and New York dazed men and horses.

Men seeking the three o'clock shade of the *Plow & Harrow* in the Bowery, City of New York, fifth day of July, 1787, were suddenly distracted from the late afternoon swelter.

(July 5, 1787)

Pulling up smartly on hot axles that brought the hostler and inn boy to the curb came a road-dusted sulky. It tilted sharply under the substantial dismounting traveler whose bearing drew notice. With authority lightened by a smile he nodded the boy to the small trunk and instructed the hostler about care of the foaming horse at the Bowery barns. With suit coat over arm he followed the baggage boy. The observers yielded a passageway as if for someone they should recognize.

Many would someday. He had come to buy a state.

The Mission And The Man

To observe the presumptuous turning of national destiny about to be attempted here in the next few days...converting 13 sovereign states to a single nation with authority for admitting and governing many new states...we need to know something of the Massachusetts man just arriving to make the largest purchase thus far on the continent.

To make this purchase he must function as a powerful salesman. He needs to persuade the faltering government to govern. And then persuade it to accept his purchase. This Congress is controlled by giant southern leaders with no love for Yankees, and the visitor will be opposed by his own Massachusetts congressmen who want him to buy land from the 30,000 square miles in Massachusetts' province of Maine.

It is not important that this Manasseh Cutler is a lawyer. Nor that he is a doctor. Nor that he is an accomplished scientist. Nor that he is a minister, nor a military man.

What becomes important in view of his mission is that he is all of these. He is in tune with several polities. That may be what Putnam knew.

Even more important and remarkable — he wears all those credentials lightly. He is confident of the world, does not battle it; he flows with it.

He has not struggled up a ladder as Putnam and Tupper. A lightning intellect brings him easy victories, permitting him to enjoy life, and others to do so in his presence. At 45, Cutler has a full head of wavy hair framing a full face and unwrinkled brow. Unguarded eyes invite relaxation in those with whom he deals. All portraitists catch the suggestion of a smile on full lips.

This is the man approaching Congress to attempt what many others have tried for seven years. However, Cutler has had much practice in the unlikely. Graduating from Yale at 23 he began trying on occupations like hats. Two years whaling out of Martha's Vineyard he found confining. He went to storekeeping.

In the dull hours he studied law. Admitted to the Massachusetts bar in 1767, he found the practice dull.

He studied theology. Ordained in 1771 at Ipswich, he ministered there until 1776 when he joined the Revolution as a chaplain.

Before war's end Cutler returned to his Ipswich parish and began the study of medicine. Receiving his M.D., he served as both minister and physician.

Meanwhile, the restless intellect discovered astronomy, meteorology and botany. Like many a brilliant man he found his church in nature. He began the first dictionary of the plants of New England, classifying 348 species. A member of the American Academy of Arts and Sciences, he was probably the equal in the learned professions of any living men in America, save perhaps Dr. Franklin and Mr. Jefferson. All that accomplishment resided in a commanding presence. "Stately and elegant in form, courtly in manners. Yet affable," is the description by a contemporary.

Cutler's relaxed manner, however, veiled precise thoroughness. On June 24th, 1787 Cutler left his home in Ipswich, Massachusetts, for New York by way of Lynn where he preached a sermon, and by way of Cambridge where he called on Dr. Willard, Harvard president, to get letters of introduction to southern congressmen. He rode to Boston with Willard to confer with several others and to meet with Putnam regarding "the principles on which I am to contract with Congress for lands on account of The Ohio Company." He also obtained letters of introduction to Putnam's old army friends now in Congress.

(June 24, 1787)

He then proceeded by way of Middletown, Connecticut, to confer two days with General Parsons. Although Parsons' land selection did not please The Ohio Company directors, nor perhaps did his presentation style to the Congress, Cutler shrewdly understood Parsons' enormous stature. Some leaders still remembered that the whole concept of a Continental Congress may have originated with Parsons. Samuel Parsons was the man The Ohio Company wanted to promote for governor of the West. Besides conferring on tactics, Cutler got from Parsons still other letters of introduction to congressmen, including the powerful Virginians, Carrington, Grayson and Richard Henry Lee.

Massachusetts Man On A Timetable

In his room at the *Plow & Harrow*, Cutler sorted out his 43 letters of introduction and reviewed them. Then he bathed, changed his clothes and "took myself a walk into the city."

(July 5, 1787)

(July 6, 1787)

Promptly on the morning of Friday July 6th, Cutler delivered some of his letters to congressmen.

He went to see Samuel Osgood, president of the Board of Treasury to spell out his proposal to purchase a million and a half acres northwest of the Ohio River for The Ohio Company.

Osgood, according to Cutler's journal..."promised to make every exertion in his power in our favor."

In a whirlwind morning Cutler then went to City Hall where Congress met. At 11 o'clock Colonel Edward Carrington introduced him around to several members on the floor of the Congress chamber. Introduction by Carrington was fortunate because, although a new member, he was trusted by southerners for courage and integrity. Captured by the British and exchanged, he became quartermaster to Greene, and was with Washington at Yorktown. (He would be jury foreman in the Aaron Burr trial.)

Cutler quickly declared to Congress his petition and proposed The Ohio Company's terms for purchase.

He had of course two missions: first — get Congress to establish governance policies for the Ohio Country as a future state of the union equal with the other 13; second — to buy an enormous tract there for The Ohio Company at a good price, and using bounty land warrants for partial payment. If Cutler succeeded, large as those goals were, there would be a sweeping consequence far beyond his objectives: the plan for governance of the whole land to the Pacific would be set.

Cutler outlined genially the land requirements and the statehood needs of The Ohio Company, and the price and terms they would like to pay.

The Congress was at that moment working on a revision to the Monroe Ordinance of 1785 which was a revision of the Jefferson Ordinance of 1784, both unworkable. The revision committee was Carrington and R. H. Lee, Dane of Massachusetts, Johnson of Connecticut, Pinckney of South Carolina, Smith of New York, and McHenry of Maryland.

The writing and wrangling of such plans could go on for years or until the British reseized the West. Getting any action through

Congress was like cutting the dark with a knife because of constant lack of quorum; delegates came and went at pleasure, and some had to shuttle 90 miles over to Philadelphia to represent their states in the Federal Convention for revising the Articles of Confederation, now recognized by the working leaders as a constitutional convention.

But here suddenly with Cutler's arrival was a huge customer for land who would buy right now...if they could provide a form of government under which the veterans he represented would agree to settle. The Congress therefore immediately formed a new committee:

Edward Carrington, Virginia (ch.)
Nathan Dane, Massachusetts
Richard Henry Lee, Virginia
Melancthon Smith, New York
John Kean, South Carolina
Rufus King, Massachusetts
James Madison, Virginia

Strangely, they named new member Carrington chairman over the heads of previous committeemen, Dane and Smith. While it might appear that a south-dominated Congress wanted southern control of this Yankee proposal, Cutler tended to be pleased. He had a rapport with the gracious southern colonel, whereas he expected opposition from salty New Englanders; and of his own townsman, Dane, he was wary. Although Cutler was a minister, he knew Dane to be a strict Puritan layman devoted to a fiercer God than Cutler perceived in his studies of nature and medicine. They were both from Ipswich, but Dane was co-founder of a temperance society, an act Cutler found unneighborly.

Committeemen King and Madison were away in Philadelphia at the Federal Convention for revising the Articles. Dane and Smith were the continuity on the committee. The latter, a former sheriff on Long Island, had a legendary memory and a powerful mind. He devoured print as some men quaff ale. Dane had a proprietary, possessive feeling for the committee's work. Harvard trained and a lawyer, his was also a powerful intellect, but with a leaning to the academic side of the law. He preferred settling his cases outside the courts. His vertical, bruise-colored face glared critically at a world which did not quite return the respect he was due.

This committee quickly started work on a better ordinance for governing the territory north and west of the Ohio River. That region cupped by the Ohio and Mississippi Rivers was named The Northwest Territory.

Cutler left the building to begin a whirlwind week, first to present some other letters of introduction in the city. He knew the broad argument for and against this huge purchase would overflow the Congress hall into the taverns, homes and offices. And he intended to be there. One of his letters of introduction was to a prominent business family, the Hendersons, who invited Cutler to use their house as headquarters.

Cutler had early supper that same day with Nathan Dane and his roommate, the Comptroller of Treasury. Then he spent the rest of the evening with several congressmen.

(July 7, 1787)

Saturday morning, Cutler met with Thomas Hutchins, geographer to the United States, to discuss locations in the Ohio Country. He was receiving invitations for the following week to teas and dinners.

(July 9, 1787)

Early Monday morning, he again sought Hutchins for more information about the land and to study maps all the way to the Illinois territory. Hutchins urged the Muskingum River area as the best. He said that the Shawnees, under pressure from Iroquois marauding the Ohio River, had withdrawn north of the Ohio shore leaving safe the forest astride the lower Muskingum. This did not seem to mesh closely with Tupper's report at the *Bunch of Grapes*.

Cutler left Hutchins early to call on the land committee before Congress opened. Then he had a second meeting with Hutchins who again pressed the Muskingum. He claimed that the Seven Ranges Indian attacks were not relevant, that survey being far enough north. That would later prove a dangerous assumption, but Cutler was convinced, and logically enough. Had not The Ohio Company's own Ben Tupper, despite the Indians on Seven Ranges, started the whole scheme on the basis of Muskingum lands?

Cutler left Hutchins to lunch with a group of clergy, which included Congressman Holton. He then walked quickly to the land committee at Congress. "Debated terms," he told his journal, "But we were so wide apart, there appeared little prospect of closing a contract."

Cutler's personality was such, however, that the congressmen wanted to show him through the whole storied building, describing its history.

In the afternoon he again consulted Hutchins about location. That evening he spent with Dr. Holton and other congressmen near the Congress hall in Hanover Square.

On Tuesday, after finding time to visit Columbia College, he dined with Osgood of Treasury and William Duer, Secretary of Treasury, noting in his diary, "Duer lives in the style of a nobleman."

(July 10, 1787)

Cutler used every social occasion to dilute some deep-rooted opposition to his proposal. For example, New England congressmen, especially Gerry, feared the draining exodus of good men to the west. Massachusetts wanted to turn migration toward its province of Maine. Southern congressmen did not want any new state to be *northern*, increasing the Yankee block. Small states feared being overwhelmed by creation of huge western states, the very battle which was deadlocking the Federal Convention over in Philadelphia.

Cutler knew that convention was also mired to a halt over whether states would be superior or inferior to the central government; and if new states were authorized, would they be equal to the old? Would they soon outnumber and outvote old states who had fought the Revolution?

The Customer

When Cutler arrived in New York the Congress was prepared to sell some parts of the Seven Ranges, but offered little that could be called a government to protect the purchaser. Cutler's group also did not want to buy into the Seven Ranges because the government would retain alternate townships there. The Ohio Company wanted to control its whole purchase.

The subject of the back country had been before Congress for years, culminating in the ineffective Ordinances of 1784 and 1785. All these plans had been made by committeemen who had no intention of going west to live. Hence the plans were theoretical. But here now were men represented by this Cutler who planned to abandon everything they had in the east to move west, staking their futures on this new land. Congress could see they needed a government in the territory, not theoretical, but practical.

Cutler used each social event to present the benefits of approving The Ohio Company purchase. Guests gave him the opportunity by clustering around this distinguished presence in the black velvet suit, black stockings and silver knee and shoe buckles. His quick wit and broad knowledge entertained in drawing room debate.

In the on-going argument he avoided direct confrontation as a cat stepping through broken glass. He abjured hammering an argument; he instead marshalled facts in a certain sequence the way some men force a card. To his hostesses and other ladies, Cutler revealed the merits of a barrier of military veterans between the Shawnees and the existing states.

It was no mere courtesy that Cutler paid close attention to the women's questions. A family man with grown children, he did not bury frank appreciation for handsome and accomplished women, noting in his journals their remarks, costumes and hairstyles.

The financially astute he tempted with the once-in-a-lifetime chance for the government to wipe out a huge part of its debt at a stroke, raising government credit by paying off the bounty land warrants.

Talking to military men, Cutler reminded them how easily Britain or France or Spain could take over the vast unoccupied west, with the assistance of the outraged Delawares, Shawnees and Wyandots now led by chiefs experienced in recruiting whites against whites.

To federalists who wanted a strong central national government to prevent indiscriminate and chaotic western settlement, Cutler pictured the thousands of squatters outrunning government, creating a lawless frontier.

In the four days following his arrival Cutler conducted a selling tour de force. The city mirrored the optimism he projected.

Despite his affability, however, he never carried himself as supplicant. He was here as a customer, the largest this Congress would ever see.

He made it clear that the principals he represented would not buy just a large tract of land. They needed land with a good government organization, land that would quickly become a state, equal in rights to the 13 originals. His message reached the committee from many sides.

The Ordinance Committee worked hurriedly, producing an ordinance and getting it quickly into one of the three required readings before Congress, which asked for some changes.

The Committee worked on these changes with unusual dispatch.

On the 11th they had a new bill ready for a second reading to Congress. They furnished Cutler a copy, inviting his suggestions or amendments. (July 11, 1787)

In making his suggested changes, Cutler put his cards on the table, even if some were face down. He wanted fair treatment of the Indians. Altruism? Yes — but also he did not want any new federal Indian policy designed by men safely ensconced in New York to stir up a Shawnee hornet's nest against Ohio Company families out in the western forests. He asked for guarantees of property rights and the sacredness of contracts. Altruism? Yes — but especially he did not want any future congress to be able to annul The Ohio Company's contract after the settlers had risked everything to move west.

It is often written that he added the concept in Article III, "Religion, morality and knowledge being necessary to good government and the happiness of mankind, schools and the means of education shall forever be encouraged." Perhaps he did. Many years later he tacitly permitted the credit, and still later answered a question about it affirmatively. However there grows around prominent men legendry easier to permit than correct. That concept appears back in the Pickering Plan and before that in the early Virginia legislation by William Blount proposing cession of Virginia lands.

Additionally, Cutler's main mission on this trip was less philosophical and more practical — buying a piece of land. As to religion:

Cutler's religion was a genial one, not heavy on the back. It seems more likely that Nathan Dane's harsh religion entered here.

Cutler completed his recommendations, returned the draft before supper on July 11th and packed a satchel for Philadelphia. The men in Philadelphia could be building a constitution which would negate the contract Cutler was attempting with the Congress in New York. They could prescribe subordinate status for western states, and undo provisions of the Ordinance.

Ideological traffic between the Philadelphia Convention and the New York Congress, both by post and in person was frequent, as some leaders shuttled between both.

At 7:00 o'clock July 11th, Cutler crossed the Hudson on the ferry to Paulus Hook and rode the stage down Old York Road into Philadelphia.

One example of the traffic in ideas between Congress and the Federal Convention is that Rufus King left the New York Congress to attend the Philadelphia Convention. Dane meanwhile kept him informed of the New York action, posting a letter July 10: "The Ohio Company appeared to purchase a large tract west of the federal lands (Seven Ranges Survey) (...) and we wanted to abolish the old system and get a better one for government of the country."

Of the many issues splitting the 55-man Federal Convention in July, three cut to whether leaders really trusted liberty. They were: how to create a representation system in a national legislature which would be fair to both the small and large states; to create a king or a president; and whether or not to create new states or colonies in the West? If states, should they be subordinate to the old states or equal?

This last argument especially concerned Manasseh Cutler. His Ohio Company colleagues did not want to buy into a second class colony with second class representation, and perhaps with no formal government to protect its property. Worst of all, the Federal Convention might make a constitution which would later be found to nullify land contracts such as The Ohio Company sought. Although the Philadelphia men were well aware of the Ordinance nearly finalized in New York, this Federal Convention could strip it.

In the middle of this battle, Manasseh Cutler came to town and signed in at the Indian Queen. The high style of Philadelphia appealed instantly to the Reverend Cutler. No spartan type religionist; he enjoyed every detail enough to record it. A ruffle-shirted, smartly-liveried boy carried up his luggage. The room, overlooking the Delaware River and New Jersey was finely furnished, including late issues of English journals. Cutler sent the boy for a barber and sat to penning a note to Caleb Strong, a Massachusetts delegate (and a future governor) who had been drafting laws for years.

As a result of the note, as in New York, the visitor quickly found himself in tavern conversation until one in the morning over aged beverage with a handful of the leadership — Mason, Rutledge, Pinckney, Madison and Hamilton.

While there was a Convention secrecy rule forbidding delegates to discuss proceedings with outsiders, Cutler, as in New York, quickly ceased being an outsider.

He had no official status or right to attend. But he could make this appearance under the highest auspices in all innocence because he previously had carried on some scientific correspondence with Doctor Benjamin Rush and Doctor Benjamin Franklin, both convention delegates. The aging Franklin mostly listened in the convention, but when he did speak from the seated position, he commanded every ear.

Delegates who met Cutler soon invited him home.

He began a whirlwind cultivation of the leadership as intensive as his New York visit. In fact, the very next morning he was up before 5:00 (people started early to escape unbearable heat) to walk with Strong to breakfast at the temporary quarters of political veteran Elbridge Gerry, the shrewd delegate whose name endures in the political glossary as gerrymander. Gerry was a financial wizard. He drafted the law in the first Continental Congress authorizing privateering as a device for acquiring a navy overnight without money. He opposed creation of equal western states to "drain our wealth."

At table, joining the discussion of national destiny, to Cutler's delight and surprise, was Gerry's beautiful young wife. Nearby was her new baby whom Cutler admired, marveling that a former old bachelor like Gerry could have such luck.

In the afternoon, Cutler went to Market Street to pay respects to perhaps the second best known American, even though his son was a Tory. Dr. Franklin, the aging sage, received Cutler with courtly humor in his garden and displayed his rare two-headed snake. Franklin was about to draw a specific parallel with the Convention when another visitor, familiar with the doctor's favorite analogy, spoiled the fun by reminding him of the convention secrecy rule. Franklin then ordered Cutler to call on him again, and prepared for a nap.

Despite that secrecy rule, Cutler received a clear tactical picture of The Ohio Company proposal's enemies and friends here.

The opponents were a capable corps which included Gerry, Nathaniel Gorham and Rufus King of Cutler's own state, and George Clymer, a Philadelphia merchant and signer of the Declaration, who said it was suicide to encourage the West. Powerful opponents against forming equal western states were also Butler, Martin, and Rutledge.

But the driving heart of the opposition was the dominant Gouverneur Morris. The West should be treated as a colony.

Morris was a match for Cutler as negotiator. While Cutler probably had an edge in sheer intellectual power, Morris commanded something perhaps even more powerful — affection. He was respected for financing the war, as assistant to Finance Superintendent Robert Morris. He was a handsome figured man (later chosen to pose for the statue of Washington) and like Cutler, an admirer of beautiful women.

Spontaneous, hearty and genial, when he thumped along a corridor and clapped a meaty hand on a delegate's shoulder, partly for support and partly in conspiratorial argument, there was a powerful pull to agree with his arguments. What could backwoodsmen in leather shirts offer in the high councils, except to start wars with Spain and prevent the states acquiring Florida and Canada? How are they going to train statesmen out in the woods to represent them equally with the eastern states?

Roughshod, Morris ignored Congress' already written ordinance guaranteeing new states equality.

Cutler also learned who were the friends of the West. One of the most intense was the never popular, always respected, James Wilson. His haughty demeanor may have been caused by his nearsightedness; the glasses low on the nose forced his head back. Primshouldered, with a bulbous chin, he had not the bearing nor personality for gregarious leadership. Nor was he loved for possessing the largest law practice in Pennsylvania. Yet in this convention full of distinguished lawyers, he was the most brilliant. His encyclopedic knowledge went back to Greece, his logic was piercing.

Delegates did not gather around him in the taverns, but when Wilson rose in the Convention to speak, the chamber hushed so quiet the flies became loud. His intellectual clarity was, as Benjamin Rush put it, a "blaze of light."

Wilson's residual Edinburgh Scottish burr attacked the premature jealousy of the eastern states against future western states. "The fatal maxims espoused by Britain were that the colonies were growing too fast, and that their growth must be stinted (...)." Then he invited the delegates to recall the results, "First enmity on our part, then actual separation." The applause when he sat down was thought-filled silence. (Later Washington would appoint him to the Supreme Court).

Madison and Mason of Virginia were also powerful advocates for equality for future western states.

Cutler's arguments for making no constitution which would limit the new western states or abrogate land sales made by Congress were by now sharply honed. One which showed his sincerity was that his own 19-year-old son definitely would be in The Ohio Company advance party and perhaps another son would follow shortly.

Campus Martius Museum, Marietta, Ohio
The Ohio Company land office

Chapter 8: The Compact

(Compact n., a solemn covenant)

When Cutler was in Philadelphia, Carrington's committee reworked the Ordinance slightly hoping to accommodate both Cutler's requests and Congress' prejudices in a second reading.

(Evening July 11, 1787)

Two changes to that draft are in the handwriting of Grayson (temporary president of Congress).

One is addenda to the provision abolishing the primogeniture custom in which the eldest son inherits everything. Grayson added, "and there shall in no case be a distinction between the kindred of the whole and half blood (children)."

The other change exempted the French settlers already in the Illinois country, allowing grandfather rights to retain their old country system of descent and conveyance of property.

Charles Thompson's handwriting changed Virginia from "authorizing" a boundary change (in land cession) to "consenting."

The Compact

Working over the language carefully on Thursday, hoping not to antagonize certain congressmen with any paragraph, the committee's big addition was in the closing section, Articles of Compact... defining largely the relationship, the compact, between any new states and the original states. In that day the word *compact* meant the most sacred promise.

(July 12, 1787)

Deep in the roots of the race is fear. And one of the most terrifying age-old fears to this day is government as bully. Hence the Articles of Compact were precious. They are the America story.

Article I assured religious freedom. Article II was a bill of rights, assuring habeas corpus (right to possession of one's own body), trial by peers, no cruel and unusual punishment, property rights and representation of the people in the legislature. It also included what Cutler demanded, a provision that no future government could annul the contract he hoped to make. That provision would later benefit millions in other contexts. The language read, "...it is understood and declared that no law ought ever to be made (...) that shall interfere with (...) private contracts (...) previously formed."

Much of Article II traced back nearly 600 years to Chapter 39 of the Magna Carta, worth repeating. Although violated brutally on mass scales by crazed despots and vicious local officials, it is man's hardest won concept. In England it read:

"No freeman shall be taken, imprisoned, disseized, outlawed, or in any way destroyed, nor will we proceed against him or persecute him, except by the lawful judgement of his peers and (...) the laws of the land."

Article III encouraged education in its opening sentence. The balance of the article responded to Cutler's mandate for fair treatment of the Indians.

Article IV required any new states to "forever remain a part of this confederacy (...) subject to the Articles of Confederation." This was to avert a new state becoming a separate nation or a province of France, England or Spain.

It covered also taxation, freedom of the waterways and the ownership of the soil.

Article V outlined the rules and boundaries and procedures for forming new states and admitting them to the union.

With those five articles completed, and approved in the second reading, the committee felt its work was done on the 12th of July.

Yet we know there were ultimately six articles. What happened?

The influential Carrington, chairman of this committee and key member of several others, was away from the committee for several hours. After the second reading on the 12th, Nathan Dane was in charge. (July 12, 1787)

Bony, tight-strung with a knife-edged face, Nathan Dane had had a precocious rise. His sense of public service was strong; so was his personal ambition. He was transcribing a clean copy of the new Ordinance with minor changes for presenting the third reading next day to Congress in committee of the whole.

There are hundreds of scholarly printed pages debating who was responsible for Article VI, the anti-slavery article.

Many credit Cutler with demanding the inclusion of this anti-slavery provision. But Cutler was not one of the fiery abolitionists; later as a U. S. congressman he twice, for pragmatic reasons voted against anti-slavery legislation. It was not that he favored slavery, but Manasseh Cutler was a political sophisticate.

Some credit Dane with authoring Article VI; others say he acted in this matter merely as committee scribe.

What appears certain is that Dane, an alumnus of the Massachusetts abolitionist hotbed, was minutely knowledgeable of the pro and anti-slavery winds in Congress.

He had to know that in 1783 the Pickering Plan had a provision against slavery in its proposed western settlement; that Virginia's deed of cession of its western claims provided for no slaving in that northwestern land; that the first draft of the Jefferson Ordinance of 1784 provided for cessation of slavery after year 1800, even though the clause was stricken by Congress.

In 1785, March 16th, Rufus King at the suggestion of Timothy Pickering offered a no slavery amendment for the Ordinance of 1784 which was sent to committee. It died there.

Nathan Dane would have a fair knowledge of which individual congressmen were for slavery and why, which were against it but usually would not vote against it, which individuals were against it and would vote against it. Above all he knew the rising desire of many to make this sale to The Ohio Company.

In a letter to Rufus King, Dane later explained that "When I drew the ordinance (...) I had no idea that the states would agree with the VIth article, prohibiting slavery, as only Massachusetts of the Eastern states was present (in committee); and therefore omitted it in the (previous) draft. But finding the House favorably disposed on this subject, after we had completed the other parts, (Author's Note: Delaware had come to Congress with two votes.) I moved this article, which was agreed to without opposition" (in committee).

Therefore, at the eleventh hour, in a precise hand, he penned to the end of the Ordinance:

ARTICLE VI

There shall be neither slavery nor involuntary servitude in the said territory otherwise than in the punishment for crimes, whereof the party shall have been duly convicted; Provided always, That any person escaping into the same, from whom labor or service is lawfully claimed in one of the original States, such fugitive may be lawfully reclaimed and conveyed to the person claiming his or her labor or service aforesaid.

(July 13, 1787)

Congress assembled Friday morning for the third reading. Only eight states were present, 18 congressmen. In passing any legislation the men in each state's delegation voted among themselves. The outcome of that vote then became the state's single vote. The oral votes of the individuals within a state's delegation were not required on the floor unless some congressman demanded it.

As the third reading of the Ordinance came up for vote, Congressman Yates of New York demanded the individual ayes and nays. Grayson, temporary president, gaveled the podium, "So ordered." The roll call began with the north.

Massachusetts. Mr. Holton? "Aye." Mr. Dane? "Aye." The state votes in favor.

New York. Mr. Smith? "Aye." Mr. Harring? "Aye." Mr. Yates? "No!" The state votes in favor.

New Jersey. Mr. Clark? "Aye." Mr. Sherman? "Aye." The state votes in favor.

Delaware. Mr Kearney? "Aye." Mr. Mitchell? "Aye." The state votes in favor.

The roll call now moved south. A lot of complex thinking and emotion could come into play. Among these votes will be some of Congress' most influential men, no less than Carrington; Grayson, temporary president; Richard Henry Lee, 55, the South's strong man here, the backbone and energy of Congress.

R. H. Lee, a signer of Declaration of Independence, was the courageous man who rose in the second Continental Congress, on June 7th, 1776 and first uttered the official resolution, "that these united colonies are, and of right ought to be, free and independent states." In his speech to the Virginia Burgesses, he proposed a ruinous tax on slavery "to put an end to that (...) disgraceful traffic."

Dane and the committee knew that many of the giant Virginia leaders, themselves large slave holders, had long opposed slavery. They might seize this opportunity to legalize their sentiments.

Virginia. Mr. Grayson? "Aye." Mr. Richard Henry Lee. "Aye." Mr. Carrington? "Aye." The state votes in favor.

The backlands of North and South Carolina would not be controlled by an ordinance governing north of the Ohio River; and further they may explicitly wish to deprive new northern states of the economic advantage of slave labor so that they cannot compete against the South in tobacco and indigo (plants of the pea family that yield a blue dye).

North Carolina. Mr. Blount? "Aye." Mr. Hawkins? "Aye." The state votes in favor.
South Carolina. Mr. Kean? "Aye." Mr. Huger? "Aye." The state votes in favor.

Georgia was an enormous land mass extending from the Atlantic to the Mississippi, heavily dependent upon slave labor. However, it was also very vulnerable. Spanish Florida bordering her south controlled the Mississippi mouth which they could close against southern trade. The presence of a settlement of military men at the Ohio River headwaters of the Mississippi watershed could protect Georgia's riverine back door.

Georgia. Mr. Few? "Aye." Mr. Pearce? "Aye." The state votes in favor.

The southern votes were unanimous!
The gavel hit the podium.
"The issue is resolved in the affirmative. Done by these States, in Congress assembled, the 13th day of July in the year of our Lord 1787, and of their sovereignty and independence the twelfth."

Manasseh Cutler was to return to New York from Philadelphia that night, Friday, July 13th, 1787 to learn whether or not he had an Ordinance.

Chapter 9. The Land Buyer

After a part day's work in Philadelphia on Friday, Dr. Cutler signed out of the Indian Queen and headed for New York. He gave himself a night's sleep in New York on July 13th. (July 13, 1787)

Saturday morning, his journal explains that he "called on members of Congress very early (...) and was furnished with the ordinance establishing government in western federal territory. It is, 'on a degree, new modeled'. The amendments I proposed have all been made, except one (...)." (July 14, 1787)

Cutler had proposed "that we should not be subject to Constitutional taxation unless (...) entitled to full representation in Congress." They refused this but granted right of representation without voting rights when first taxed. Cutler decided to fall back on this point and save his fire for larger battles ahead.

The seventeen Americans who voted for this ordinance created the world's greatest plan for settlement and governance of a vast land mass. It was as far as we know the first plan for bringing colonies into a nation on an equal basis, and the first time a national character was established by law instead of by the character of human leaders.

If they could now implement it by agreeing on a contract which The Ohio Company would sign, they had made a *code for America*.

The Ohio Company offer to purchase land and the Ordinance of 1787 were parts of the same transaction. Cause and effect.

Forceful Virginia committee member, Richard Henry Lee, dispatched a note to General Washington at Philadelphia on July 15th, "I have the honor to enclose to you an ordinance which we have just passed in Congress for establishing a temporary government beyond the Ohio as a measure preparatory to the sale of lands."

What relays of men had been trying to accomplish in all the years since the Revolutionary War was accomplished suddenly in eight days since Cutler came to town.

If implemented by a contract with The Ohio Company, that sheet of paper could set the procedures and motivate the formation of who knew how many states? Otherwise, it could become one more musty folio in a government drawer.

Now Congress balked.

The passage of the Ordinance was only prefatory to Cutler's main mission...to buy the land.

He now pressed the Congress to approve his purchase proposal. That opened chaffering over price, terms of payments, time for occupancy, transference of the deed to the land, and who should pay survey costs.

Cutler repeated to the Board of Treasury The Ohio Company's desired terms: $500,000 payable now, $500,000 when the lines were surveyed; the balance to be paid in six equal installments computed from the date of completion of the survey by the National Geographer. The university site, Cutler argued, should be located as nearly as possible in the center of the acreage covered by the *first* payment, not the center of the entire tract. And the deed for the 1½ million acres should be given to The Ohio Company as soon as a million dollars had been paid.

Right of entry on part of the tract...immediate.

Soldiers' bounty land warrants should be accepted by the government for the amount of land on the face of the warrant, not discounted as in the open market.

Seller Resistance

Now as the negotiation hardened down from philosophy to finance, Congress complained. The payment plan was too slow. The desired occupation was too quick. The allowance of free government land for a university too large. And that university should be placed in the center of the whole purchase, not in the center of the part covered by the first payment.

Massachusetts would still prefer The Ohio Company buy land in its Maine province.

Some congressmen began to point out that the actual price came down to only about 66 cents per acre, too cheap, considering the price paid for it in blood.

Congressmen Few, Bingham and Reamy were the stubborn nucleus of the opposition.

Others complained that The Ohio Company was expecting to pay for these lands with bounty land warrants which had dropped in value sometimes to 20 cents per acre and the final certificates which, although rising some in value, were still passing in trade for under 20 cents on the dollar. So the actual price the government would be getting would be robbery.

When confronted with that argument on social occasions Cutler genially countered, is it not fine to be able to wipe out a whole dollar's worth of government debt by redeeming a piece of paper only actually worth a fraction?

When confronted by the same objection by a civilian congressman he agreed, turning the point — how fine to be able to pay the veteran closer to what was promised him rather than only a fraction?

Cutler knew that he faced one severe problem of personal politics. He had told congressmen that when a governor for the Northwest Territory was appointed, The Ohio Company would like it to be its own respected shareholder, General Parsons. However, Cutler's sensitive ear picked up the implication that General Arthur St. Clair, aloof president of Congress, coveted that post and was withholding support of The Ohio Company contract because of Parsons.

Some congressmen worked changes into the contract. The price should be a full hard money dollar an acre, allowing 33⅓ cents off for bad lands. The government should not accept bounty land warrants at face value except on one seventh of the purchase because warrants brought no cash to the treasury. No deed should be given until all payments had been made. The payment installments should not stretch out as proposed, but be paid as soon as surveyors complete the outside line.

Although he was not privy to Congress' committee sessions, Cutler's peripatetic social circuit gave him echoes of these rising objections. By the same channels he sent back messages, hinting that The Ohio Company principals might not be adamant about the appointment of Parsons as governor if the payment plan were approved as proposed.

Col. Duer Approaches

The contract continued to fall short of Ohio Company requests. However land speculators noticed Cutler's thus far great success in getting action from Congress. His aura of a man bound for higher places attracted followers.

Hence, a surprise developed. While Cutler was negotiating for the million and a half government acres, he was approached by Col. William Duer with a proposition of a private nature. Duer, officially Secretary of the Board of Treasury, was in private life also a canny man with a dollar. He had assembled a group of investor associates, "leading men in the city" and as it turned out, some leaders in Congress. They had organized "The Scioto River Project" for which they would like a very large tract in the same general region north of the Ohio River. Would Cutler include the Duer Scioto group in The Ohio Company Contract, expanding The Ohio Company's order by asking for an option on an additional several million acres on the same terms...but...keeping the Scioto group identity "a profound secret?"

Cutler, being a sophisticate of the world, recognized another, and so was cautious. He would have to think about it. Duer said his group might be able to lend The Ohio Company $100,000 to help with the down payment.

Cutler still wanted to think about it. What he actually did was confer with colleague Winthrop Sargent, a man who was alerted whenever any foot moved in the New York political or commercial spider web.

Major Sargent, 34, was complex and cosmopolitan. Traveling Europe in 1775, he returned in time to join in the defense of Boston. Rising to captain of artillery he distinguished himself in the battle of Monroeville Court House and sartorially throughout the war. Even at ragged Valley Forge his uniform was notable.

Like Cutler, in any group he was noticed. However, his aristocratic bearing was unrelieved by Cutler's type of relaxed geniality. The handsome side-burned profile was a cold ceramic cameo. His tailoring and linen were expensive, his knowledge of the polity extensive. (He would become governor of the Mississippi Territory.)

Together Cutler and Sargent considered some politics. Accepting the proposal would enlist Duer's considerable influence at Treasury and with some reluctant congressmen. More important, it would suddenly put into Cutler's hands more final certificates and bounty land warrants, making him a still larger creditor of the government, increasing his leverage enormously.

Over oysters and bracing grape juice, Cutler met Duer again in Brooklyn. Without losing affability, Cutler reined back enthusiasm. Duer then enriched his proposal; the Scioto group could perhaps lend The Ohio Company nearly $140,000 for a down payment, if that would help.

Cutler left the table agreeing to consider this.

Making use of this new leverage at his disposal, he now returned to the Board of Treasury and said that if the Congress could approve The Ohio Company purchase terms as proposed, his principals now felt they might be willing to extend the purchase substantially — several million more acres.

This appealed to those congressmen who were deeply concerned with reducing government debt. They urged approval.

Other investor groups wishing to buy land with final certificates or bounty land warrants, sensed that Cutler was a very effective negotiator with the Congress. They asked him to function as agent for them as well, connecting their land purchases to The Ohio Company tract. This lengthened Cutler's lever once more, giving

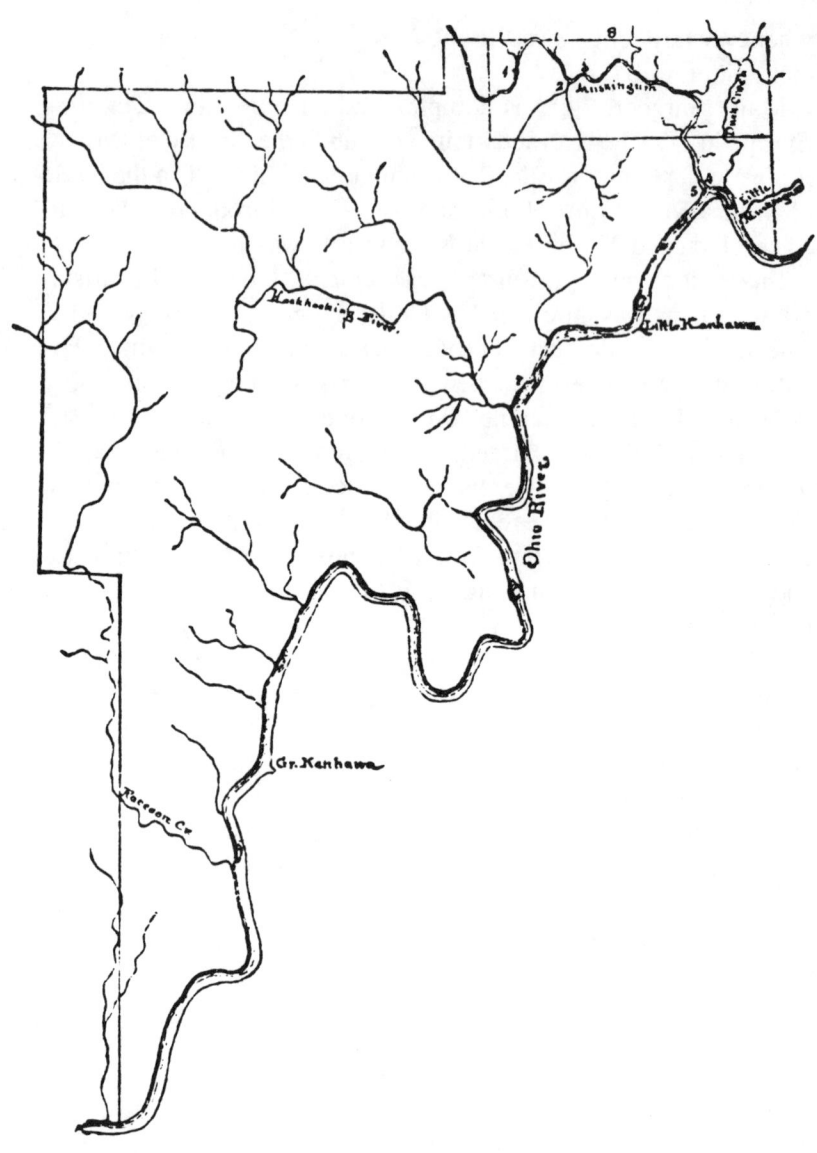

This is a sketch of the Ohio Company's purchase

him control of $7,000,000 of the confederation's debt. He became the government's largest creditor.

The Congress badly needed financial help; its entire revenue equaled less than one third of the interest it owed on its debts.

Therefore, on July 19 the committee confronted Cutler with modified terms, hoping they would please him. They had relented on the university lands, changing the language of the contract to: "(...) two complete townships be given in perpetuity for the purpose of a university, to be laid off by the purchaser." However, the new terms did not include several of Cutler's requests.

"I Propose to Leave the City"

Maintaining his affability, but also his posture as the government's largest potential customer, he courteously thanked them for all their work. Then he spoke as a man saying all there is to say, "but acting for the best interests of (...) my principals," he would need to "try to purchase the lands from some of the states (which) would give incomparably better terms." And therefore he proposed to "leave the city immediately." (July 19, 1787)

He paid his parting respects around town as he noted in his journal "to all members of Congress in the city," and informed them of his "intention to depart (...) and (...) turn his attention to some other parts of the country."

One more day ticked into history.

On July 20th several congressmen called upon him asking that he stay; they felt Congress was in a mood to give better terms. Cutler appeared indifferent and turned the conversation to the advantages of a contract with one of the states. "This I found had the desired effect." (July 20, 1787)

A delegation of congressmen called on Cutler the next day suggesting that he not be hasty. Cutler elected to spend another high card. He told them that, "(...) if Congress would accede to the terms of my proposal, I would extend the purchase from the 10th township from the Ohio and to the Scioto, inclusively, by which Congress could pay more than four million of the public debt." (July 21, 1787)

At this same meeting Cutler made another powerful argument: it was the Ohio Company's "intention to secure (...) most robust and industrious people in America (...) which must immediately advance the value of federal lands (adjacent) (...) and prove an important acquisition to Congress."

The contract was debated "warmly" until 3 o'clock on July 23rd.

(July 23, 1787)

Cutler spent the evening with Col. Grayson and members of Congress from the South. He used this social occasion for some blunt politics, "If General Parsons could have the appointment of first judge and Sargent, secretary, we could be satisfied." He pointed out that General St. Clair could then be governor of the Northwest Territory, and, "I would solicit eastern members (of Congress) to favor such an arrangement."

They asked Cutler what appointment he would like for himself. He said none, but he would like to see Rufus Putnam made one of the three territorial judges of the territorial legislature.

(July 24, 1787)

The following day Cutler received from the Board of Treasury a revised contract, asking if he would be willing to close on those terms. As the contract was now much larger than when he was acting only for The Ohio Company, he asked Sargent to join him in studying the contract.

Hence the 24th of July finds Cutler again writing out more advantageous terms and forwarding them to the Board of Treasury. The government should survey the lands at its own expense, not the buyer's. There were certain changes in the payment schedule. Section 16 in each township should be for the support of free schools, section 29 for the ministry in addition to the two townships for the university.

(July 25, 1787)

These requests stiffened the opposition. Manasseh Cutler properly gauged its strength, and he now employed all the friends he had made. In his words, "Every machine in the city that it was possible to set to work, we now set in motion (...) to win over my opponents. In order to get at some of them so as to work powerfully on their minds, we were obliged to engage three or four persons before we could get at them. In some instances we engaged one person who engaged a second, and he a third and so on and so forth.

"In these maneuvers I'm much beholden to Colonel Duer and Major Sargent."

On the street at 11:00 o'clock in the morning Cutler and Sargent were greeting the congressmen who were entering the hall when General St. Clair strode along, aloof, very British, the very image of a senior officer reviewing troops on parade, long after the parades were over.

(July 26, 1787)

He saw Cutler and abruptly his aloofness melted. He told Cutler and Sargent that he would "make every exertion to prevail with Congress to accept the terms contained in the letter."

However, he told them they must expect opposition. The most vigorous opponents remained Bingham, Few and Reamy. Cutler's journal estimated, "Of Few and Bingham there is hope, but to bring over that stubborn mule of Reamy is beyond our power."

Cutler assessed his chances with other legislators. Strangely he remained unsure of the support of his fellow Ipswich townsman, Nathan Dane. Yet he was hopeful of other support. "The bearer of treasury I think will do us much service if Dr. Lee (not Richard Henry Lee) is not against us, though Duer assures me I have the length of his foot, and he calls me a frank, honest New England man, which he considers an uncommon animal. Yet from his zealous cautious make, I feel suspicious of him, especially as M. Osgood tells me he has made every attempt to learn his sentiments, but is unable to do so."

Cutler dined that night with Sir John Temple and others; but left abruptly to call on Dr. Holton to get a report on the day. He learned that Congress spent the whole day warmly debating the contract, "but our friends did not think it prudent to call for the vote lest there should not be a majority in our favor."

Cutler was very discouraged and told Dr. Holton it was useless to "wait any longer and should certainly leave the next day."

Holton exclaimed against Cutler's impatience. If Cutler accomplished his objective a month later, it would still "be far more expeditious than was common in getting much smaller matters through Congress." Holton said this was "of great magnitude for it far exceeded any private contract ever made before in the United States."

Cutler noted in his journal, "To comfort me he assured me on his honor that he never knew so much attention paid to any one person who made application to them on any kind of business. He could not have supposed that any three men from New England, even of the first character, could have accomplished so much in so short a time. This I believe was mere flattery, though (...)"

Cutler learned that Bingham had come over, but Few and Reamy were still stubborn.

Unfortunately there were only eight states represented and unless seven of them approved, the contract could not pass. "Every moment of this evening until 2:00 o'clock was busily employed. A warm siege was laid on Few and Reamy from different quarters and the attack is to be renewed in the morning."

Duer, Sargent and Cutler agreed upon an emergency plan, if needed, "Sargent will go on to Maryland which is not at present represented, and prevail on the members from that state to come on and interest themselves (...) in our plan. I am to go on to Connecticut and Rhode Island to solicit members from those states to go to New York and to lay anchor to windward of them. As soon as these states are represented, Sargent is to renew the application and I have promised Duer that if necessary I will return to New York again."

(July 27, 1787)

Cutler arose and packed his baggage. "For I was determined to leave New York this day. I set out on general morning visits, paid my respects to all members of Congress, and informed them of my intention to leave the city that day. My expectations of forming a contract I told them were nearly at an end. I would however await the decision of congress and (...)." If unfavorable, Cutler said he would look to the states for land at half the price.

Even at this last farewell he gave a powerful argument about the possibility of Spain taking over the west if the land was not settled, and that if this contract were not approved, Congress would probably thereby turn away offers from others to colonize the west.

The aggressive, earnest Richard Henry Lee assured Cutler in his deep Virginia-flavored accent that he was going to make a one hour speech, and expected to win. R. H. Lee had the respect of

Congress. He was on that famous committee which wrote the letter to the King of Great Britain in 1774, putting himself in danger. All urged Cutler to stay.

"But I assumed an air of perfect indifference and persisted in my determination, which had apparently the effect I wished. Passing the city hall as the members were going in to Congress, Col. Carrington told me he believed Few was secured. That little Reamy was left alone, and that he (Carrington) was determined to make one trial of what he could do in Congress."

As it was believed to be Cutler's last day in New York, Mr. Henderson (his host) insisted on his staying for dinner with a number of invited friends.

At Half After 3:00 O'Clock

Slightly after midday Congress directed the Board of Treasury, "take the order and close the contract."

At half past three Cutler was informed that the terms of his letter had been approved "without the least variance."

"Sargent and I went immediately to the Board of Treasury, who had received the ordinance, but were then rising (quitting work). They urged me to tarry the next day and they would put all business aside to complete the contract, but I found it inconvenient, and after making a verbal adjustment, left it with Sargent to finish."

Cutler proposed three months for collecting the first half million dollars, which was granted.

He wrote in his journal: "By this ordinance we obtained the grant of nearly 5,000,000 acres of land amounting to 3½ million dollars, one million and a half acres for The Ohio Company and the remainder for private speculation (the Duer group and others)." He wrote that without the Duer addition, the contract could not have been negotiated.

At half past six Cutler took leave of his hosts. He went to the Bowery horse barns and ordered out his sulky. This time the people chatting at the curb knew by name the man who had come to buy a state.

(July 30, 1787)

With the Ordinance of 1787 pocketed, he snapped the reins for Middletown, Connecticut.

There Cutler found General Parsons not the least disturbed at not being named Governor of the Northwest Territory. Territorial judge suited him. He proposed writing his friends in Congress to appoint Cutler as one of the three judges.

Cutler declined.

He rehitched, and headed for Massachusetts to tell Rufus Putnam.

The Ohio Company purchase would not have been made without the Ordinance. And the Ordinance could not have been enacted without the offer to purchase.

But as the sulky rolled northeast, Cutler, being a student of the world and its history, had to wonder if the paper ordinance he brought north would really convert to action when it came right down to time to pack wagons.

When it actually came time for action, would the veterans break away from these pine-flavored hills and salt-scented coasts? Would aging, spider-bellied shareholders actually ask wives to live in dirt-floor log huts 800 miles from friends, relatives and grandchildren?

Could Putnam and Tupper leadership surmount those barriers at the moment of truth?

How well did he really know Putnam?

Chapter 10: Company Business

Cutler had reason to worry whether the piece of paper in his pocket would translate to action. Even as he worked his sulky north, copies of Congress' Ordinance were under study by the Federal Convention at Philadelphia where some important provisions were incorporated into the proposed Constitution.

However, despite full knowledge of the Ordinance's provision for equal status for new states, Gouverneur Morris and his corps of supporters continued fighting it. They ultimately caused the delegates to drop from the proposed Constitution the provision that new states "should be admitted on the same terms as the original states."

However, Rufus King, no friend of western development but an attorney with a solid sense of good law, successfully proposed a resolution adapted from the Ordinance of 1787 that *"no law ought ever to be made, or have force in said territory, that shall, in any manner whatever, interfere with, or affect private contracts or engagements (...) previously formed."* That should save The Ohio Company's contract. This appears in Article 1, Section 10, Clause 1 of the Constitution, said to be the first enactment of its kind in constitutional law.

Finally the Constitution left to the Congress the disposal of lands and responsibility to "make all needful rules (...) respecting the territories (...) belonging to the United States."

In the case of The Ohio Company purchase, the Congress had already done that, and the Company had in hand the contract. And the Ordinance guaranteed honoring contracts.

That contract was being reviewed for The Ohio Company directors and agents, August 29, in the *Bunch of Grapes* in Boston. Cutler explained to the directors the boundaries of the land for which he had contracted. East boundary was the western line of the seventh range of the Seven Ranges Survey. South boundary, the Ohio River. West boundary, a meridian drawn north from the western cape of the Great Kanawha River. The north boundary was a line at right angles to the 7th range at the bottom of Township 3 running west to intersect the west boundary.

The directors fully approved, ratified, and confirmed Cutler's work.

The group elected General James Varnum to the board of directors and elected Colonel Richard Platt of New York City, treasurer.

The news was announced that some of the Ohio country Indians were challenging the right of their chiefs to sign away their lands, but the mood of the moment was not to worry about it.

On the next day the group voted that a tract of 5,760 acres at the confluence of the Muskingum and Ohio Rivers be reserved for a city and a commons.

The members prepared the details of the settlement move.

(November 21, 1787)
In a November meeting at *Cromwell's Head* tavern, Boston, directors resolved that "house lots shall consist of 90 feet front, 128 feet in depth." They resolved to meet again the first Wednesday in March, 1788, to draw lots for the eight-acre farm lots which they expected to be surveyed by that time. Eight acres is a very small farm indeed. Putnam fought this, saying that 64 acres ought to be the minimum farm. But others voted him down on the grounds that an owner could buy as many eight acre lots as he wished and that a man would find eight acres all he could handle when clearing ancient trees said to measure 30 to 40 feet around at the butt.

(November 23, 1787)
Two days later at Bracket's Tavern in Boston the company resolved that four surveyors be employed, that 22 men attend these surveyors, that there be added to the party 22 more men including boat builders, four house carpenters, one blacksmith, nine common workmen. Forty-eight men in all. These employees could be shareholders, but need not be.

"The boat builders to proceed at once on Monday next to the

Youghiogheny River to construct transports to convey the first party to the Muskingum."

Putnam was elected superintendent of settlement. Plans were made for 100 houses to be built on three sides of a square.

Each man was to furnish himself a rifle, bayonet, six flints, powder horn, pouch, half pound of black powder, one pound of balls and one of buckshot.

The surveyors were to be paid $27 a month, laborers $4.00 and board.

While the first task on the western site would be the construction of a village, this was no village mentality. The Ohio Company shareowners were senior officers and soldiers of the Revolution and Harvard and Yale graduates. They were not going west merely to start a town. They were going west to start the Northwest Territory.

One of their members, Winthrop Sargent, was by this time officially Secretary of the Territory. Three of the shareowners comprised the appointed legislature of three territorial judges: Generals Parsons, Varnum and Putnam.

Rufus Putnam had reached the age when most men of affairs pull back their empire boundaries to within the picket fence around a rose garden. But now as superintendent of settlement, he and his party, would precede the newly appointed territorial governor into the region.

The aging general would begin his largest mission. As senior American official in the field he would launch the Northwest Territory as acting governor — in the face of a rising confederation of Shawnees, Delawares, Wyandots and British.

Dayton-Montgomery County Public Library
Winthrop Sargent

Chapter 11: Putnam

Smoking at the nostrils, the horses turned rumps to late November blowing in off the Atlantic. The oxen locked to the canvas-covered wagon, stomped slush, enduring the farewell speech of the Reverend Doctor Manasseh Cutler. Suddenly ears and hides flickered at the blast of ceremonial rifles.

(November 30, 1787, Ipswich Mass.)

Before the burnt powder scent blew away, the drover put the silk to the team and the party of a dozen trudged toward Danvers, Massachusetts, beside a wagonload of tools, weapons and provisions under the black canvas that announced their presumption — "For The Ohio Country."

Cutler had supplied the wagon, the lettering and the sense of mission.

In this party were 12 men, boat builders and mechanics, including shipwright Jonathan Devol (who would later build tall ships for service down the Mississippi and across the Atlantic). Cutler's son, Jervis, was in the group. His two other sons, Temple and Ephraim, planned to go later.

At Danvers they rendezvoused with another group, making 22 in all. Under Major Haffield White this party headed west.

The plan was for them to cross Massachusetts, New York and Pennsylvania to Sumrill's Ferry on the Youghiogheny River, southeast of Ft. Pitt. There, they were to build flatboats to carry the whole party down the Yo to the Monongahela to the Ohio River, and down the Ohio to the mouth of the Muskingum.

The other team of the advance party, 26 men, rolled west out of Hartford, Connecticut New Year's day with the four surveyors who would mark out the city and plat The Ohio Company's lands. The surveyors were the 6'4" giant, Col. Ebenezer Sproat, assisted by three younger men, Return J. Meigs, John Matthews, and Benjamin Tupper's son, Anselm.

Young Tupper and Matthews had worked the Seven Ranges Survey under Benjamin Tupper and Thomas Hutchins, and so knew the territory. Meigs had not, but the future governor of Ohio was a scholarly young man who would catch on quickly. This party was to join Major White's boat builders on the Yo. Hopefully the boats would be ready.

Rufus Putnam was in charge of this Connecticut group, but he suddenly had urgent need to go to the War Department in New York to acquire copies of the relevant Indian treaties. Therefore, he put the giant Ebenezer Sproat in charge, with orders to travel. Putnam would catch up with them at Swatara Creek between Harrisburgh and Lebanon, Pennsylvania.

Sproat's deep voice dinned like a dray horse stomping through a covered bridge, "Forward. And keep the animals warm."

(January 23, 1788)

Major White's party of boat builders out of Danvers took the old military road across William Penn's state, threaded the Allegheny hills carefully, making it to Sumrill's Ferry in eight weeks, arriving January 23rd.

They began to build two large boats.

(January 24, 1788)

Putnam picked up the applicable Indian treaties in New York and overtook Sproat's party of surveyors at Lincoln's Run near Swatara Creek at the base of the Tuscorora Mountains. He found them at a standstill shut down by weather. A broad creek they needed to cross was frozen, but not enough to support the wagon.

In pinch-nostril cold, Putnam put the men to chopping passage through the ice, requiring a full day. That day and the next so much snow fell that it took five days trudging up the foothills of the Tuscorora Mountains to an accommodation which later became Strasburgh. Here they learned that nothing had crossed the mountains since the new snow, and in the old snow, a foot deep, only pack horses had crossed. No wagons.

Driving snow blew out the sun in places, making it hard to see snow-filled washouts. Ascending the mountain slaunchwise to keep from slipping, horses sometimes sank chest-deep in gullies. The climb seemed impossible. But veterans down to their last chance were too scared not to try. They talked up the horses and strained on the ropes.

But higher in the mountains the horses could not move the supply wagon. It seemed they would have to wait for the melt. Putnam sat like a moulting owl, studying the wagon. They needed to get to the territory early enough to clear timber and get seed down. With his eye on history's clock, Putnam ordered men to build sleds.

With the horses and sleds single file and the men breaking snow in front, they made the climb. Then with the loom of the hills at their backs, they began the descent. Holding back on the sleds, they came down into Sumrill's Ferry.

The boat building half of the party had arrived there long since, but had shut down boat construction.

Putnam knew, however, that if the new colony were to survive and feed men and animals, they must get onto their new land by early spring. With the infusion of the extra men and horses, plus a certain emphatic approach that Putnam brought, boat construction resumed despite snow.

The largest flat boat shaping up on blocks was an unshiply square galley 50' x 13' (some say 45' x 12') scow-bowed and roofed high enough to shelter standing men and animals. Theoretical capacity was 21 tons if you allow nothing for the weight of green timber.

Some called it *The Adventure Galley.* Putnam's diary called it the *Union Galley,* an apt name if it succeeded in creating a new state for the union. Historical sentimentalism entered the picture, however, and it came to be called the *Mayflower.*

Putnam dispatched young Matthews down the Ohio River to Buffalo Creek with some cash to buy flour, dried beans and corn.

(February 27, 1788)

The second large flatboat rising on the shore of the Youghiogheny was 28' x 8', the Adelphia. The walls of this floating fort contained defensive gun slits and were thick enough to stop lead balls and stone-tipped arrows.

Even though General Varnum previously had made a formal peace pipe and whiskey treaty clearing Indian title on the north bank of the Ohio, only a handful of Shawnee and Delaware chiefs really understood the white man's pentracks on parchment, and they were already eager to forget them. The whiskey was gone, as was the sentiment.

In addition to these flatboats the men built three large canoes.

The troughs in the snow darkened with spring's waters running under the crust. Putnam urged speed.

As March ran down, the boats lay ready for side launch. April burned snow off the mountains; the Youghiogheny rose, lifting the starboard sides of the *Union Galley* and the *Adelphia*. Devol barked to loose the port side lines and all hands push.

The *Adelphia* slipped her moorings first, then the little fleet floated down the Youghiogheny into the Monongahela, down that to the Ohio River with a cargo for colonization.

On extra high waters they floated downstream between shores already turning spring yellow.

They steered ashore at the mouth of Buffalo Creek on the Virginia side to take aboard John Matthews and the provisions at this last stop short of the Shawnee hunting grounds.

(April 5, 1788)

As they floated southwest the men scanned the shore for Indian signs and grew quieter. The gurgle and lap of waters on the boats whispered mystery as Yankees saw a different kind of landscape, forest so dense it held a piece of the night all day.

(April 7, 1788)

The eighth day afloat came on wet. Rain speckled the river and mist obscured the shore. The surveyors serving as navigators knew they should be getting close to the mouth of the Muskingum. But the way the sycamores leaned out from both banks of tributaries concealed the mouths.

As they floated by Ren's Island, Captain Devol told Putnam, "I think it's time to take an observation. We must be near."

So The Ohio Company overshot the east bank of the mouth of the Muskingum, but discovered it early.

The canoes could come about and paddle back upstream, but there was no way to propel the large boats back upstream against the current.

They steered for shore landing a little downstream of Ft. Harmar high above them on a cliff where Harmar School now stands. Major Doughty of Ft. Harmar dispatched troops to the river bank. They grabbed the lines and pulled the large boats back upstream to the mouth of the Muskingum. Jervis Cutler and Amos Porter jumped ashore before the bow touched.

There was of course exuberant greeting between The Ohio Company men and the Ft. Harmar troops. There was cordial introduction to 70 Wyandots and Delawares and the chief, Captain Pipe. Yet the Yankees and the red men studied each other thoughtfully.

Northwest Territory

The boats were later tied to the east bank of the Muskingum near its confluence with the Ohio. On that point of ground Rufus Putnam's boots sucked mud as he and Colonel Sproat strode over the land and envisioned the town layout. They ordered the erection of Putnam's old headquarters tent, plundered from Burgoyne at the British surrender.

They carried ashore timbers they had brought for temporary huts. And they stayed.

With his mind on the corn planting calendar, Putnam immediately ordered clearing, seeding and surveying. And he began construction of defensive works, 60 chains in from the Ohio and eight chains in from the Muskingum. It would be a fortress, Campus Martius, and none too soon.

The clearing was shoulder-wracking labor. Putnam measured one tree 44½ feet around; another revealed 465 rings. Axes nibbled at the ancient oaks like toys.

The falling monsters bounced on the ground, spraying up snapped branches and clouds of scolding grackles, the fragrance of fractured oak mixed with the powerful acrid scent of new earth stabbed open by falling jagged branches thick as a man's trunk.

Trees in the path of future outlying installations were only girdled to die slowly.

Amid the physical tumult were gentler matters of the mind as men began putting names on the streets and the institutions of this city and state they were building.

Considering that the leaders in convention in Philadelphia termed this the "back country," the names the settlers selected had a seeming comedic grandeur...Rome, Troy, Carthage, Sacra Via, Capitolium, Campus Martius. For such grand street names to be tacked pretentiously onto wagon wheel ruts in the woods gave chuckles to some later chroniclers who had not had opportunity for study of the identities of these men.

While there were some "hired laborers" in the crew, The Ohio Company shareholders were not the storybook frontiersmen simply seeking family farms. They included senior army officers and field grade and company grade officers and experienced soldiers who had come to create a state.

To the surprise of many, The Ohio Company of Associates was also the largest concentration of Harvard and Yale graduates ever to colonize a piece of America; and they had come down the river bearing a special ordinance enabling them to create no fewer than three or more than five states. For them to call upon the grand names of history — Rome, Carthage, Troy — was natural.

And when they established Ohio University on the land grant authorized by the Ordinance, it was natural they named the town Athens.

Because the Ordinance required that the state initiate establishing the university, they had to wait until the state was created, and then a few years more.

Finally a red brick building rose three stories with white trim and a cupola on top. The first building — Cutler Hall. Today it stands dead center of a great university. As the president's administration office, it has directed the higher education of generations of Americans in and beyond the Territory.

Washington said of these Ohio Company settlers, "No colony in America was ever settled under such favorable auspices as that just commenced on the Muskingum. (...) I know many of the settlers personally, and there never were men better calculated to promote the welfare of such a community."

With each ancient tree the settlers felled in 1788, they opened up great patches of sky. By July these first axemen had let in enough sun to raise corn knee high; so there was time for longer thoughts of government until St. Clair should arrive to govern. Putnam was still working out of Burgoyne's old tent.

To a beech tree in front of that tent General Benjamin Tupper, who had arrived later, carried a parchment containing 13 handwritten rules for the colony. Some were for the defense. Some were for the mind, one providing for reading and learning. But Number 13 announced:

Be it further ordained that the Metropolis be named Marietta, in honor of Queen Marie Antoinette of France who gave aid (...) during the darkest days of the Revolution.
Rufus Putnam

The names of the first and second groups are given in the appendix. Wives and children began coming later in the same year. Studying the names is an historical adventure because many of these settlers would ultimately move out north and west of Marietta. Many of the men were each the type who is a community in himself, and wherever you put him, he would build one. Hence we find their names throughout the Northwest Territory on streets and creeks, towns and cities and forts.

They were followed by others bearing the same parchment, Ordinance of 1787; and they put other names on the land: Detroit, Chicago, Milwaukee, Ohio, Indiana, Illinois, Michigan and Wisconsin — a region as large as the Mediterranean world named in the streets of Marietta.

And these were followed by others who, on the design outlined by the same parchment, created Minnesota, Nebraska, Wyoming, California — and so on to 50 United States, united largely because when the nation stood on a pivot that could be tipped by a feather, the great ordinance tilted it to nationalization, expedited completion of a constitution, and opened the proving ground for the United States of America.

Index

Adams, John Quincy, 34, 49, 69
Adelphia, 112
Adventure Galley, 111
Annapolis Convention, 65
Articles of Confederation, 17, 43, 64, 66, 68, 70, 77, 88

Bingham, 95, 101, 102
Bounty Lands, 27, 28, 37, 48, 52, 58-62, 76, 80, 94, 95, 97
Bracket's Tavern, 60, 106
Brooks, John, 60
Bunch of Grapes Tavern, 59, 78, 106
Bunker Hill, 35
Burr, Aaron, 20, 76, 85

Campus Martius, 113, 114
Carrington, Edward, 22, 75-77, 87, 88, 91, 103
Chase, Samuel, 43, 49
Clymer, George, 20, 84
Congress, 16-21, 23, 25-30, 33, 34, 37-39, 41, 43-45, 48-51, 61, 62, 65, 66, 70, 73-83, 85, 87, 89-97, 99-105
Cornwallis, 16, 25
Crocker, Sampson, 60
Cushing, Thomas, 60
Cutler, Ephraim, 109
Cutler, Jervis, 109, 113

Cutler, Manasseh, 22, 60-62, 70, 71, 73-85, 87-89, 92-97, 99-106, 109, 114
Cutler, Temple, 101, 109

Dane, Nathan, 22, 50, 76-78, 82, 89-91, 101
Dayton, Jonathan, 68
Devol, Jonathan, 109, 112
Duer, William, 79, 96, 97, 101-103

Education, 21, 29, 81, 88, 115

Few, 92, 95, 101-103
Fort Edwards, 34
Fort Finney, 56
Fort Harmar, 51, 113
Fort McIntosh, 53, 55, 56
Fort Meigs, 110
Fort Ticonderoga, 34, 36
Franklin, Benjamin, 20, 68, 69, 75, 83, 84

Gerry, Elbridge, 20, 45, 71, 79, 83, 84
Gorham, Nathaniel, 84
Grayson, 75, 87, 90, 91, 100
Greene, General, 30, 76

Habeas Corpus, 21, 22, 50, 88
Hamilton, Alexander, 17, 21, 66, 68, 70, 83
Henry, John, 50

Holton, Dr. 79, 90, 101
Howe, General, 35, 36
Howell, David, 43-45, 49
Hutchins, Thomas, 55, 56, 78, 79, 110

Jefferson, Thomas, 41, 43-45, 48, 49, 69, 75, 76, 89
Johnson, William S., 49, 50, 76

Kean, John, 49, 50, 77, 91
King, Rufus, 20, 41, 45, 49, 50, 68, 71, 77, 82, 84, 89, 105
Knox, Henry, 15, 16, 36, 67, 68

Lee, Arthur, 48
Lee, Richard Henry, 22, 75-77, 91, 93, 101, 102

Marietta College, 18
Madison, James, 17, 64-66, 68, 69, 77, 83, 85
Magna Carta, 18, 22, 88
Martin, Luther, 20, 84
Mason, George, 68, 83, 85
Matthews, John, 110-112
Mayflower, 111
Mills, John, 34, 60
Monroe, James, 41, 43, 48-50, 66, 76
Morris, Gouverneur, 19, 68, 69, 71, 84, 85, 105
Morris, Robert, 84
Muskingum River, 51, 61, 78, 106, 107, 109, 112, 113, 115

Newburgh, 25, 27, 28, 38
Northwest Territory, 18, 47-49, 78, 95, 100, 104, 107, 113, 115

Ohio Company of Associates, 18, 19, 21, 58, 60-62, 70, 75, 76, 79-82, 84, 85, 89, 93-97, 100, 103-107, 113-115
Ohio University, 114
Ordinance of 1784, 43, 45, 48, 76
Ordinance of 1785, 50-53, 61, 76, 82
Osgood, Samuel, 76, 79, 101

Parsons, Samuel H., 56, 61, 75, 95, 96, 100, 104, 107
Patterson, John, 60
Pickering, Timothy, 25-31, 37-39, 45, 52, 62, 81, 89
Pinckney, Charles, 49, 50, 68, 76, 83
Pipe, Captain, 56, 112, 113
Platt, Richard, 106
Plow & Harrow, 73, 75
Primogeniture, 21, 87
Putnam, Israel, 33
Putnam, Rufus, 33-38, 53, 55, 57-62, 74, 75, 104, 106, 107, 109-113, 115

Randolph, Edmund, 17, 66-68
Reamy, 95, 101-103
Rush, Benjamin, 83, 85
Rutledge, Edward, 20, 68, 83, 84

St. Clair, Arthur, 95, 100, 101, 115
Sargent, Winthrop, 60, 61, 96, 97, 100-103, 107
Seven Ranges Survey, 17, 26, 33, 37, 51-53, 55, 56, 58, 59, 74, 78, 79, 82, 102, 106, 110
Shays, Daniel, 15
Shays' Rebellion, 65
Slavery, 21, 29, 43, 44, 47, 89-91
Smith, Melancthon, 50, 76, 77, 90
Spaight, Richard, 41, 43-45, 62
Sproat, Ebenezer, 110, 113
Stewart, Col. Robert, 27
Strong, Caleb, 83
Sumrill's Ferry, 109-111

Thompson, Charles, 18, 87
Tupper, Anselm, 55, 110
Tupper, Benjamin, 53, 55-61, 74, 78, 104, 110, 115

Union Galley, 111, 112

Varnum, James M., 106, 107, 112

Washington, George, 15-17, 19, 21, 25, 26, 28, 30, 31, 33-38, 43, 47, 49, 58, 64-70, 76, 84, 85, 94, 115

Wayne, Gen. Anthony, 37
White, Maj. Haffield, 109
Williams, Abraham, 60
Wilson, James, 85

Yorktown, 15, 22, 68, 76
Youghiogheny River, 107, 109-112

Other Relevant Reading

The following are suggested not for original scholarship work, but for readability and availability for the interested layman and student.

The most compact comprehensive coverage is still probably the 95-page *History of the Ordinance of 1787 and the Old Northwest Territory,* prepared in 1937 for the Northwest Territory Celebration Commission, Harlow Lindley, Chairman, Norris F. Schneider, Milo M. Quaife.

Nearly as comprehensive is the account in Vol. II of *History of the State of Ohio* (6 Volumes), edited by Carl Wittke, published 1941 by Ohio State Archaeological and Historical Society.

Unmatched for human interest details after the landing at Marietta is Samuel P. Hildreth's, *Biographical and Historical Memoirs of Early Pioneer Settlers,* Cincinnati, 1852.

A volume which many find most readable and informative is by Mary Cone, *Life of Rufus Putnam with Extracts from His Journals and an Account of the First Settlement in Ohio,* W. W. Williams Company, Cleveland, Ohio, 1886.

Many volumes in the Ohio Historical Society quarterlies contain short pieces on different aspects of the Ordinance. Those volumes are included in the list below.

* * *

Benjamin William Arnett. "The Northwest Territory." *(Ohio Archaeological and Historical Publications,* Vol. VIII, pp. 433-463). Published by Frank J. Heer for the Society, Columbus, Ohio, 1900.

Jay A. Barrett. *Evolution of the Ordinance of 1787.* Arno Press and New York Times.

Catherine Drinker Bowen. *Miracle at Philadelphia, The Story of the Constitutional Convention, May to September, 1787.* (An Atlantic Monthly Press Book) Little, Brown and Company, Boston, Massachusetts, 1966. Very little about the Ordinance, but excitingly told.

Edwina Buell, ed. *Memoirs of Rufus Putnam.*

Jacob Burnet. *Notes on the Early Settlement of the Northwest Territory.* Derby, Bradley and Company, Publishers, Cincinnati, Ohio, 1847. Burnet was personally involved in territorial government.

Andrew R. L. Cayton. *The Frontier Republic, 1780-1825.* Kent State Press, 1986.

Nannie McCormick Coleman. *The Constitution And Its Framers.* The Progress Company, Chicago, Illinois, 1910. This volume gives good personal portraits of those men who were framing both the Ordinance and the Constitution.

Judge Joseph Cox. "The Building of the State." *(Ohio Archaeological and Historical Publications,* Vol. II, pp. 143-165). Published by Fred J. Heer for the Society, Columbus, Ohio, 1888.

Manasseh Cutler. *Diaries and Papers of Manasseh Cutler.*

William P. Cutler. "The Ordinance of July 13, 1787." *(Ohio Archaeological and Historical Publications,* Vol. I, pp. 10-36). Published by Fred J. Heer for the Society, Columbus, Ohio, 1887. The author was a direct descendant of Manasseh Cutler.

William P. Cutler and Julia Perkins Cutler. *The Life, Journals and Correspondence of Rev. Manasseh Cutler, LLD.* (two volumes) First published in 1888, reprinted in 1987 by The Ohio University Press.

Major E. C. Dawes. "The Beginning of the Ohio Company and the Scioto Purchase." *(Ohio Archaeological and Historical Publications,* Vol. IV, pp. 1-29). Published by Fred J. Heer for the Society, Columbus, Ohio, 1896.

James Thomas Flexner. "The Trumpet Sounds Again." *American Heritage Library.* American Heritage Publishing Company, New York, April, 1969, Volume XX, pp. 65-73. A gripping picture of Washington deciding whether to attend the Constitutional Convention.

Douglas Southall Freeman. *George Washington, A Biography. (Patriot and President,* Volume Six). Charles Scribner's Sons, New York, 1954.

Only a brief reference to the Ordinance, but interesting.

C. B. Galbreath. "The Ordinance of 1787, Its Origin and Authorship." *(Ohio Archaeological and Historical Publications,* Vol. XXXIII, pp. 110-175). Published by Frank J. Heer for the Society, Columbus, Ohio, 1925.

Honorable W. J. Gilmore. "Address Delivered at Greenville, Ohio, August 3, 1895." *(Ohio Archaeological and Historical Publications,* Vol. VII, pp. 241-255). Published by Frank J. Heer for the Society, Columbus, Ohio.

"The Ordinance of 1787: Some Investigations as to the Authorship of the Famous Sixth Article." *(Ohio Archaeological and Historical Publications,* Vol. XIV, pp. 148-157). Published by Frank J. Heer for the Society, Columbus, Ohio, 1905.

Frank M. Johnson. *The Rectangular System of Surveying.* Government Printing Office, Washington, D.C., 1924.

George P. Knepper. *An Ohio Portrait.* Ohio Historical Society, Columbus, Ohio, 1976.

Clement L. Martzloff. "Ohio University - The Historic College of the Old Northwest." *(Ohio Archaeological and Historical Publications,* Vol. XIX, pp. 411-455). Published by Frank J. Heer for the Society, Columbus, Ohio, 1910. This piece details one important result of the Ordinance, higher education.

"Address at Marietta, Ohio 1858, by Honorable Thomas Ewing." *(Ohio Archaeological and Historical Publications,* Vol. XXVIII, pp. 186-207). Published by Frank J. Heer for the Society, Columbus, Ohio, 1919.

"The Memorial Structure at Marietta." Report of a Committee of the Society, *American Archaeological and Historical Publications,* Vol. II, pp. 212-223. Published by Frank J. Heer for the Society, Columbus, Ohio, 1888.

"Ohio Valley Historical Society: Minutes of Ninth Annual Meeting, October 21-22, 1915." *(Ohio Archaeological and Historical Publications,* Vol. XXV, pp. 157-259). Published by Frank J. Heer for the Society, Columbus, Ohio.

"Ordinance of 1787." *(Ohio Archaeological and Historical Publications,* Vol. V, pp. 50-57). Published by Frank J. Heer for the Society, Columbus, Ohio, 1897.

William E. Peters. *Ohio Lands and Their Subdivision.* William E. Peters, publisher, Athens, Ohio, 1918. This concerns strictly the surveying of the land. Technical.

William F. Poole. An article in *North American Review*. April, 1876. Excellent coverage of Manasseh Cutler's work.

S. V. Proudfit. *Public Land System of the United States Historical Outline*. Government Printing Office, Washington, D.C., 1924.

Rufus Putnam. *Rufus Putnam Papers,* including *Journals of Rufus Putnam*. Microfilm at Brigham Young University Library, Provo, Utah 84602.

Emilius O. Randall and Daniel J. Ryan. *History of Ohio, The Rise and Progress of an American State*. (Volume Five). The Century History Company, New York, 1912.

Emilius O. Randall. "Editorialana: Jefferson's Ordinance." *(Ohio Archaeological and Historical Publications,* Vol. XX, pp. 118-133). Published by Frank J. Heer for the Society, 1911.

"Rutland - 'The Cradle of Ohio' - A Little Journey to the Home of Rufus Putnam." *(Ohio Archaeological and Historical Publications,* Vol. XVIII, pp. 54-77). Published by Frank J. Heer for the Society, Columbus, Ohio, 1909.

Daniel J. Ryan. "The Scioto Company and Its Purchase." *(Ohio Archaeological And Historical Publications,* Vol. III, pp. 109-139). Published by Frank J. Heer for the Society, Columbus, Ohio, 1895.

Dwight L. Smith, ed. *The Western Journals of John May*. Historical and Philosophical Society of Cincinnati, 1961.

William F. Swindler. "The Letters of Publius." *American Heritage Library*. American Heritage Publishing Company, New York, June, 1961, Volume XII, Number 4, pp. 4-7.

John Randolph Tucker. "Oration of Honorable John Randolph Tucker, LL.D." *(Ohio Archaeological and Historical Publications,* Vol. V, pp. 60-82). Published by Frank J. Heer for the Society, Columbus, Ohio, 1888. The fact that this is a speech does not make it thin on facts. A good reference.

John L. Vance. "The French Settlement and Settlers of Gallipolis." *(Ohio Archaeological and Historical Publications,* Vol. III, pp. 45-81). Published by Frank J. Heer for the Society, Columbus, Ohio, 1895. This is an aside, yet relevant and dramatic.

David K. Watson. "The Early Judiciary of Ohio." *(Ohio Archaeological and Historical Publications,* Vol. III, pp. 141-159). Published by Frank J. Heer for the Society, Columbus, Ohio, 1895.

The Northwest Ordinance

(July 13, 1787)

An Ordinance for the Government of the Territory of the United States northwest of the River Ohio.

[Sec. 1.] Be it ordained by the United States in Congress assembled, That the said Territory, for the purposes of temporary government, be one district, subject, however, to be divided into two districts, as future circumstances may, in the opinion of Congress, make it expedient.

[Sec. 2.] Be it ordained by the authority aforesaid, That the estates, both of resident and non-resident proprietors in the said territory, dying intestate, shall descend to, and be distributed among, their children, and the descendants of a deceased child, in equal parts, the descendants of a deceased child or grandchild to take the share of their deceased parent in equal parts among them; and where there shall be no children or descendants, then in equal parts to the next of kin in equal degree; and among collaterals, the children of a deceased brother or sister of the intestate shall have, in equal parts among them, their deceased parents' share; and there shall in no case be a distinction between kindred of the whole and half blood; saving in all cases to the widow of the intestate her third part of the real estate for life, and one-third part of the personal estate; and this law relative to descents and dower, shall remain in full force until altered by the legislature of the district. And until the governor and judges shall adopt laws as hereinafter mentioned, estates in the said territory may be devised or bequeathed by wills in writing, signed and sealed by him or her in whom the estate may be (being of full age,) and attested by three witnesses; and real estates may be conveyed by lease and release, or bargain and sale, signed, sealed, and delivered by the person, being of full age, in whom the estate may be, and attested by two witnesses, provided such wills be duly proved, and such conveyances be acknowledged, or the execution thereof duly proved, and be recorded within one year after proper magistrates, courts, and registers shall be appointed for that purpose; and personal property may be transferred by delivery; saving, however, to the French and Canadian inhabitants, and other settlers of the Kaskaskies, Saint Vincents, and the neighboring villages who have heretofore professed themselves citizens of Virginia, their laws and customs now in force among them, relative to the descent and conveyance, of property.

[Sec. 3.] Be it ordained by the authority aforesaid, That there shall be appointed from time to time by Congress, a governor, whose commission shall continue in force for the term of three years, unless sooner revoked by Congress; he shall reside in the district, and have a freehold estate therein in one thousand acres of land, while in the exercise of his office.

[Sec. 4.] There shall be appointed from time to time by Congress, a secretary, whose commission shall continue in force for four years unless sooner revoked; he shall reside in the district, and have a freehold estate therein of five hundred acres of land, while in the exercise of his office. It shall be his duty to keep and preserve the acts and laws passed by the legislature, and the public records of the district, and the proceedings of the governor in his executive department, and transmit authentic copies of such acts and proceedings, every six months, to the Secretary of Congress. There shall also be appointed a court to consist of three judges, any two of whom to form a court, who shall have a common-law jurisdiction, and reside in the district, and have each therein a freehold estate in five hundred acreas of land, while in the exercise of their offices; and their commissions shall continue in force during good behavior.

[Sec. 5.] The governor and judges, or a majority of them, shall adopt and publish in the district such laws of the original States, criminal and civil, as may be necessary and best suited to the circumstances of the district, and report them to Congress from time to time, which laws shall be in force in the district until the organization of the general assembly therein, unless disapproved of by Congress; but afterwards the legislature shall have authority to alter them as they shall think fit.

[Sec. 6.] The governor, for the time being, shall be commander-in—chief of the militia, appoint and commission all officers in the same below the rank of general officers; all general officers shall be appointed and commissioned by Congress.

[Sec. 7.] Previous to the organization of the general assembly the governor shall appoint such magistrates and other civil officers, in each county or township, as he shall find necessary for the preservation of the peace and good order in the same: After the general assembly shall be organized, the powers and duties of the magistrates and other civil officers shall be regulated and defined by the said assembly; but all magistrates and other civil officers not herein otherwise directed, shall, during the continuance of this temporary government, be appointed by the governor.

[Sec. 8.] For the prevention of crimes, and injuries, the laws to be adopted or made shall have force in all parts of the district, and for the execution of process, criminal and civil, the governor shall make proper divisions thereof; and he shall proceed, from time to time, as circumstances may require, to lay out the parts of the district in which the Indian titles shall have been extinguished, into counties and townships, subject, however, to such alterations as may thereafter be made by the legislature.

[Sec. 9.] So soon as there shall be five thousand free male inhabitants, of full age, in the district, upon giving proof thereof to the governor, they shall receive authority, with time and place, to elect representatives from their counties or townships to represent them in the general assembly: Provided, That, for every five hundred free male inhabitants, there shall be one representative, and so on, progressively, with the number of free male inhabitants, shall the right of representation increase, until the number of representatives shall amount to twenty-five; after which the number and proportion of representatives shall be regulated by the legislature: Provided, That no person be eligible or qualified to act as a representative, unless he shall have been a citizen of one of the United States three years, and be a resident in the district, or unless he shall have resided in the district three years; and, in either case, shall likewise hold in his own right, in fee-simple, two hundred acres of land within the same: Provided, also, That a freehold in fifty acress of land in the district, having been a citizen of one of the States, and being resident in the district, or the like freehold and two years' residence in the district, shall be necessary to qualify a man as an elector of a representative.

[Sec. 10.] The representatives thus elected shall serve for the term of two years; and in case of the death of a representative, or removal from office, the governor shall issue a writ to the county or township, for which he was a member, to elect another in his stead, to serve for the residue of the term.

[Sec. 11.] The general assembly, or legislature, shall consist of the governor, legislative council, and a house of representatives. The legislative council shall consist of five members, to continue in office five years, unless sooner removed by Congress; any three of whom to be a quorum; and the members of the council shall be nominated and appointed in the following manner, to wit: As soon as representatives shall be elected the governor shall appoint a time and place for them to meet together, and when met they shall nominate ten persons, residents of the district, and each possessed of a freehold in five hundred acres of land, and return their names to Congress, five of whom Congress shall appoint and commission to serve as aforesaid; and, whenever a vacancy shall happen in the council, by death or removal from office, the house of representatives shall nominate two persons, qualified as aforesaid, for each vacancy, and return their names to Congress, one of whom Congress shall appoint and commission for the residue of the term; and every five years, four months at least before the expiration of the time of service of the members of council, the said house shall nominate ten persons, qualified as aforesaid, and return their names to Congress, five of whom Congress shall appoint and commission to serve as members of the council five years, unless sooner removed. And the governor, legislative council, and house of representatives, shall have authority to make laws in all cases, for the good government of the district, not repugnant to the principles and articles in this ordinance established and declared. And all bills, having passed by a majority in the house, and by a majority in the council, shall be referred to the governor for his assent; but no bill, or legislative act whatever, shall be of any force without his assent. The governor shall have power to convene, prorogue, and dissolve the general assembly, when, in his opinion, it shall be expedient.

[Sec. 12.] The governor, judges, legislative council, secretary, and such other officers as Congress shall appoint in the district, shall take an oath or affirmation of fidelity, and of office; the governor before the President of Congress, and all other officers before the governor. As soon as a legislature shall be formed in the district, the council and house assembled, in one room, shall have authority, by joint ballot, to elect a delegate to Congress, who shall have a seat in Congress, with a right of debating, but not voting, during this temporary government.

[Sec. 13.] And, for extending the fundamental principles of civil and religious liberty, which form the basis whereon these republics, their laws and constitution are erected; to fix and establish those principles as the basis of all laws, constitutions, and governments, which forever hereafter shall be formed in the said territory: to provide, also, for the establishment of States, and permanent government therein, and for their admission to a share in the Federal councils on an equal footing with the original States, at as early periods as may be consistent with the general interest.

[Sec. 14.] It is hereby ordained and declared by the authority aforesaid, That the following articles shall be considered as articles of compact between the original States and the people and States in the said territory, and forever remain unalterable, unless by common consent, to wit:

Article I
No person, demeaning himself in a peaceable and orderly manner, shall ever be molested on account of his mode of worship or religious sentiments, in the said territory.

Article II
The inhabitants of the said territory shall always be entitled to the benefits of the writs of habeas corpus, and of trial by jury; of a proportionate representation of the people in the legislature, and of judicial proceedings according to the course of the common law. All persons shall be bailable, unless for capital offences, where the proof shall be evident, or the presumption great. All fines shall be moderate; and no cruel or unusual punishments shall be inflicted. No man shall be deprived of his liberty or property, but by the judgment of his peers, or the law of the land, and, should the public exigencies make it necessary, for the common preservation, to take any person's property, or to demand his particular services, full compensation shall be made for the same. And, in the just preservation of rights and property, it is understood and declared, that no law ought ever to be made or have force in the said territory, that shall, in any manner whatever, interfere with or affect private contracts or engagements, bona fide, and without fraud previously formed.

Article III
Religion, morality, and knowledge being necessary to good government and the happiness of mankind, schools and the means of education shall forever be encouraged. The utmost good faith shall always be observed towards the Indians; their lands and property shall never be taken from them without their consent; and, in their property, rights, and liberty, they shall never be invaded or disturbed unless in just and lawful wars authorized by Congress; but laws founded in justice and humanity shall from time to time be made, for preventing wrongs being done to them, and for preserving peace and friendship with them.

Article IV
The said territory, and the States which may be formed therein, shall forever remain a part of this Confederacy of the United States of America, subject to the Articles of Confederation, and to such alterations therein as shall be constitutionally made; and to all the acts and ordinances of the United States in Congress assembled, conformable thereto. The inhabitants and settlers in the said territory shall be subject to pay a part of the federal debts contracted, or to be contracted, and a proportional part of the expenses of government to be apportioned on them by Congress, according to the same common rule and measure by which apportionments thereof shall be made on the other States; and the taxes for paying their proportion shall be laid and levied by the authority and direction of the legislatures of the district, or districts, or new States, as in the original States, within the time agreed upon by the United States in Congress assembled. The legislatures of those districts or new States, shall never interfere with the primary disposal of the soil by the United States in Congress assembled, nor with any regulations Congress may find necessary

for securing the title in such soil to the bona-fide purchasers. No tax shall be imposed on lands the property of the United States; and, in no case, shall non-resident proprietors be taxed higher than residents. The navigable waters leading into the Mississippi and St. Lawrence, and the carrying places between the same, shall be common highways, and forever free, as well to the inhabitants of the said territory as to the citizens of the United States, and those of any other States that may be admitted into the confederacy, without any tax, impost, or duty therefor.

Article V
There shall be formed in the said territory, not less than three nor more than five States; and the boundaries of the States, as soon as Virginia shall alter her act of cession and consent to the same, shall become fixed and established as follows, to wit: The western State in the said territory shall be bounded by the Mississippi, the Ohio, and the Wabash Rivers; a direct line drawn from the Wabash and Post Vincents, due north, to the territorial line between the United States and Canada; and, by the said territorial line to the Lake of the Woods and Mississippi. The middle State shall be bounded by the said direct line, the Wabash from Post Vincents to the Ohio, by the Ohio, by a direct line, drawn due north from the mouth of the Great Miami, to the said territorial line, and by the said territorial line. The eastern State shall be bounded by the last mentioned direct line, the Ohio, Pennsylvania, and the said territorial line: Provided, however, And it is further understood and declared, that the boundaries of these three States shall be subject so far to be altered, that, if Congress shall hereafter find it expedient, they shall have authority to form one or two States in that part of the said territory which lies north of an east and west line drawn through the southerly bend or extreme of Lake Michigan. And, whenever any of the said States shall have sixty thousand free inhabitants therein, such State shall be admitted, by its delegates, into the Congress of the United States, on an equal footing with the original States, in all respects whatever; and shall be at liberty to form a permanent constitution and State government: Provided, the constitution and government, so to be formed, shall be republican, and in conformity to the principles contained in these articles, and, so far as it can be consistent with the general interest of the confederacy, such admission shall be allowed at an earlier period, and when there may be a less number of free inhabitants in the State than sixty thousand.

Article VI
There shall be neither slavery nor involuntary servitude in the said territory, otherwise than in the punishment of crimes, whereof the party shall have been duly convicted: Provided, always, That any person escaping into the same, from whom labor or service is lawfully claimed in any one of the original States, such fugitive may be lawfully reclaimed, and conveyed to the person claiming his or her labor or service as aforesaid,

Be it ordained by the authority aforesaid, That the resolution of the 23rd of April, 1784, relative to the subject of this ordinance, be, and the same are hereby repealed, and declared null and void.

Done by the United States, in Congress assembled, the 13th day of July, in the year of our Lord 1787, and of their sovereignty and independence the twelfth.

SCHOOL LIBRARY
90-196

90-196

973.3
Ell   Ellis, William Donohue
        The Ordinance of 1787 :
        the nation begins

DATE DUE			
MAR 11 '93			

SCHOOL LIBRARY

Oh 14   89

St Mary School Library